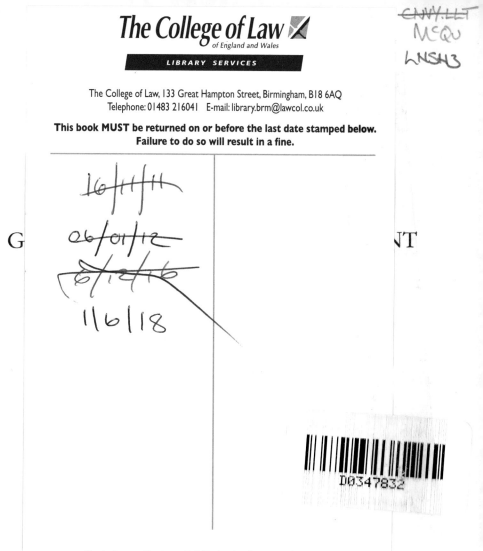

The College of Law
of England and Wales

LIBRARY SERVICES

The College of Law, 133 Great Hampton Street, Birmingham, B18 6AQ
Telephone: 01483 216041 E-mail: library.brm@lawcol.co.uk

**This book MUST be returned on or before the last date stamped below.
Failure to do so will result in a fine.**

G JT

16/11/11
06/01/12
6/12/16
1/6/18

Birmingham • Chester • Guildford • London • Manchester • York

Emerald Publishing
www.straightforwardco.uk

Emerald Publishing
Brighton BN2 4EG

© 2009 Straightforward Publishing

British Cataloguing in Publication data. A catalogue record is
available for this book from the British Library.

ISBN 9781847161048

Printed in the United Kingdom by GN Press Essex

Cover Design by Bookworks

CONTENTS

Introduction

This Revised Edition of Emerald Home Lawyer, Guide to Landlord and Tenant Law, is a wide-ranging and comprehensive book dealing with all aspects of the law as it governs the relationship between people and the ownership and tenancy of land.

The relationship between landlord and tenant has always been complex and has changed immeasurably over the centuries, particularly in the 20th century, with the huge social changes that have transformed the structure of the ownership of land. Gradually, the law has provided more and more protection for the tenant, eroding the privileges of the main land owning classes.

This brief book covers the main areas of landlord and tenant law and all of the requisite Acts. The general nature of tenancies is covered, along with the main obligations of landlord and tenant. Repairing obligations and assignments are covered in depth. Each area is highlighted by key case law.

The main Housing Acts are covered in depth along with business tenancies and agricultural tenancies. So too is the law concerning service charges and also extension of leases and purchase of freeholds.

Since the first edition appeared a major piece of legislation has been passed., The Housing and Regeneration Act 2008. The provisions of this Act are still being enacted but are wide ranging, having a bearing on tenancy law, service charges and freeholds and accommodation for gypsies and travellers, amongst other areas. It is intended to incorporate these changes in the next edition of this book.

Although no book covering landlord and tenant law can be totally comprehensive, as the subject area is vast, this particular book attempts to cover the main areas that both the layperson and the student of law need to know.

1

Outline of the Law

The law of landlord and tenant deals with the relationship, or the legal rights and obligations that arise between people when they form a relationship that is connected to land.

Defining estates in land

There are two types of estates in land which are recognised by the law. These are:

1) An estate in fee simple absolute in possession
2) A term of years absolute.

An estate in fee simple absolute in possession

This rather long-winded term means essentially a freehold estate. The holder of fee simple absolute has an unlimited amount of time on the land. This is the closest thing to absolute ownership of land that is allowable under law. The holder of a fee simple absolute is entitled to carve up the land and create smaller estates for fixed periods of time.

A term of years absolute

A term of years absolute is an estate of fixed duration, i.e. a 125 lease which expires after the duration of this period. A term of years absolute is usually known as a leasehold estate. Whenever a term of years absolute is carved out of a freehold estate the relationship of landlord and tenant arises.

Classes of occupier

Land can be occupied by a person or persons in a number of ways. There are four broad categories of occupation:

- Freehold ownership. As stated, this is where the whole estate is owned indefinitely.
- Tenant. Where a person or persons own an estate for a fixed amount of time
- Licensee. This is where a person is given permission to use the land for a period of time.
- Trespasser. This is where someone simply moves into a premises and occupies illegally.

These are the four categories of occupier at common law. Every occupier falls into one of these categories. When dealing with any type of landlord and tenant problem the first step is to determine to which category of occupier a person(s) belong.

The majority of housing Acts deal with the category of occupier who is a tenant or lessee and not with the other categories, freeholder, licensee or trespasser.

Freehold ownership

The freeholder has the strongest estate in land with the freedom to carve other estates out of it. Witness the great London estates of Governor or Cadogan. Through aristocratic privilege they own great tracts of freehold land in London and have carved other estates in land out of these freeholds. This is the basis of their wealth. However, as we shall see these estates are under attack through the leaseholders right to enfranchise and to extend leases. The occupier who owns the freehold is, in principle, the most secure of all owners with the greatest amount of rights. The estate is unlimited in time; there is no landlord with a superior interest who can reclaim the property or exercise rights over the tenant. There are outside bodies that can exercise power, such a local authorities, with planning powers and compulsory purchase powers. However, on the whole the freeholder is in the most powerful position.

Tenant

The second class of occupier, the tenant or leaseholder has lesser rights than a freeholder but is, nevertheless protected by a strong body of law, the statutory codes, Housing Acts and Landlord and

Tenant Acts. For a tenancy to come into existence the following elements must be present:

a) There must be a landlord and tenant
b) There must be exclusive possession;
c) There must be identifiable land
d) The grant must be for a definite period;
e) The lesser must retain a reversion.

For any lease to be created there must be separate legal persons capable of granting ad receiving a tenancy. The parties to the tenancy need not be individuals, any 'legal person' such as a corporate entity can grant or receive a tenancy. A tenancy can also be granted to a group of people as joint tenants. A minor, under 18, is not legally entitled to hold an estate in land. Neither is a body which does not in itself have a legal personality. An owner of land cannot grant a tenancy to himself although a director of a company can be a tenant of that company. The company or partnership has a separate legal identity to the tenant.

Exclusive possession
This is a fundamental concept. It is fundamental to any tenancy that the tenant must have been granted a sufficient degree of control over the premises for the tenant to be able to lawfully exclude anyone else from those premises, even the freeholder. The tenant will still have exclusive possession if the landlord retains a restricted right to enter the premises for a specific purpose, as is often the case, such as for inspecting the state of repair.

Exclusive possession is an essential requirement for a lease. If the occupier does not have exclusive possession, the right to use the premises does not amount to a lease, although there may be a lesser right to use.

Definition of land
The premises which are the subject matter of the tenancy must be clearly defined.

Term certain

A lease must be granted for a period that is definite. The beginning and the end must be clearly identifiable or capable of being identified. A lease can therefore be for a few days or a thousand years. The most important thing is to be able to identify clearly the term. One such case which highlights this is where a right of occupation held for the duration of the war was held not to be a lease (Lace v Chantler 1944, KB 368)

The duration of a term is not always expressed clearly. There is a distinction, which will be discussed further on, between a fixed term, a specific number of years or months and a periodic tenancy which will run from week to week or month to month and can be determined by notice.

The reversion

For a lease to be created it is essential that the term created is less than that held by the landlord. Although, as we have seen the freeholder can grant a term which is of any length as they have an unlimited duration, a leaseholder can also grant a further lease, as long as it is less than the term of their own lease. Therefore, a leaseholder with a 125 year lease can grant a 124 year lease, the main principle being that it is of a lesser term than the head lease. If the leaseholder sought to grant a lease of 125 years or more then he would have no reversion, i.e. the lease would not revert to him. There would be no rights and obligations outstanding and therefore there would be no relationship of landlord and tenant. The person granted an under lease for the same length of time as the head lease would be in effect assigning his lease.

Rent

Rent as such is not a requirement of a lease. Section 205 of the Law of Property Act 1925 defines a lease as a term of years, 'whether or not at a rent'. One case which highlights this principle is Ashburn Anstalt v Arnold (1988) 2 WLR 706. It was held that an agreement giving an occupier exclusive occupation for a certain term created a tenancy despite the fact that no rent was payable under the agreement. However, it is usual that a rent is paid under a tenancy, particularly periodic tenancies. One famous case which defined the meaning of tenancy was Street v Mountford (1985) AC 809. Whilst rent is not an essential requirement of a tenancy it is essential in order to bring that tenancy within the protection of the Rent Acts.

Owner Occupation

In the strict sense of the term only a freeholder is an owner-occupier as he or she owns the estate in fee simple absolute. Although it is common to term leaseholders as owner-occupiers this is not strictly true as a relationship exists between the freeholder and leaseholder and the freeholder retains a reversion.

Commonhold

The Commonhold and Leasehold Reform Act, an immensely important Act, which we will discuss in more depth later, introduced a new form of occupation, that of Commonhold. It is now possible for a number of occupants of separate flats to own the freehold of their own property right at the outset and also later through creation of Commonhold where leases cease to exist. Although it is possible for a group of leaseholders to purchase a freehold and form a company to manage it, nevertheless they still remain leaseholders, Commonhold creates the situation whereby all flat dwellers are freeholders, or Commonholders.

Commonholders still face restrictions on their rights to occupy parts of property. Commonholds are now in force and one of the first schemes is through a housing association and a developer in Milton Keynes.

Licensees

When an occupier is granted a licence he or she is not given an estate in land but only permission to occupy which can be withdrawn on reasonable notice. The existence of a licence makes a person's presence on the land lawful, as opposed to a trespasser. Licences vary from bare licences where permission is implied, such as friends entering a house or children of adult age staying with you to a more formal licence which, in some cases can be built into a full contract akin to a tenancy. This is known as a contractual licence. Nevertheless it is still a licence and does not imply or impute an estate in land. In the case of bare licences payment can be made but a tenancy is still not created as there was no intention to create legal relations (Hannaford v Selby (1976) 239 EG 811). A fundamental feature of the bare licence is that it can be revoked at any time and the licensee has a reasonable time to leave the premises. Once that period has expired then that person becomes a trespasser. In Robson v Hallett (1967) 2 QB 939 Police Officers knocked on the door of a house. They had no warrant or other authority to enter and were therefore merely implied licensees of the householder. The householder withdrew permission. The court implied into the licence that the officers should be given a reasonable time to leave the premises by the most appropriate route.

One point which has become pertinent is what is the meaning of 'reasonable time'. In the case of family members this can mean as much as six months. (Hannaford v Selby). Where land was occupied under licence for a long period, in this case 26 years, 12 months was seen as a reasonable time (E&L berg Homes Ltd v Gray (1980) 253 EG 473.

Trespassers

A person becomes a trespasser whenever he or she enters the land or premises of another without permission. A burglar is clearly a trespasser. Anyone who does not have permission to be on another's land is a trespasser. From the point of view of a landlord, who, having reserved a right to enter a premises to inspect for disrepair, enters a premises to harass a tenant and interfere with their possessions, the landlord becomes a trespasser if he or she has no right to enter the premises.

Commonly, a trespasser will enter a premises for a short period of time. However, over the last few decades the act of 'squatting' has gained currency. In the eyes of the law a squatter is simply a type of long-term trespasser. In Mcphail v Persons, Names Unknown (1973) Ch 447 Lord Denning defined a squatter as 'one who without any colour of right, enters an unoccupied house or land, intending to stay there as long as he can'. Usually, if a premises is found to be squatted then a court order will be obtained to evict the squatters.

****

2

Obligations in Leases

When a landlord and tenant relationship is created, a series of obligations will arise, usually *express* and *implied* obligations. The promises that are made by landlord and tenant will define a lease and create the relationship between the parties. Many of the express covenants will also be implied so, in cases where they are not expressly stated in the lease, they will seen to be implied, such as covenants for quiet enjoyment and covenants to pay rent.

Express obligations

Obligations and rights in a lease are contractual and these will arise as a result of express agreement between the landlord and tenant.

Express covenants

Covenants are the terms of contract between landlord and tenant. However, a covenant cannot be truly equated to a contractual term as a covenant can continue to impose rights and obligations on people who have acquired an interest in land after the original parties to the agreement have sold up and moved on. In this way, covenants can be said to 'run with the land'.

What distinguishes a covenant from a condition are the consequences that flow from the breach of the covenant.

Express covenants, which will be discussed below, will commonly include:

a) Landlords covenants
   1) a covenant for quiet enjoyment
   2) a covenant to repair

3) a covenant to insure
4) a covenant allowing the tenant to renew the tenancy or to purchase the landlords interest

Quiet enjoyment

This is usually an express covenant within a lease. However, even if it is not expressly set out in the agreement it will be an implied covenant. All that is required for an implied covenant is that there be a contract between landlord and tenant. A covenant for quiet enjoyment protects the tenant from interference with the most fundamental of his or her rights as a tenant-the right to exclusive possession. Of all the obligations, express or implied it is of the most importance practically in that it covers a number of situations ranging from harassment to disrepair.

One thing a covenant for quiet enjoyment cannot usually do is to provide a remedy for noise pollution. It is a misnomer that quiet enjoyment means noise free enjoyment whereas it does not. It means, essentially, enjoyment without interruption of possession.

However, if noise from a landlord is so excessive that it prevents the tenant's enjoyment of possession it could be deemed a breach of the covenant for quiet enjoyment (Sampson v Hodson-Pressinger (1981) 3 all ER 710).

Acts which amount to interference with quiet enjoyment

Usually it is thought that there has to be some physical interference, for example when a landlord engaged in mining activities underneath a property which caused the house to subside (Markham v Paget 1908)Ch697). Or where a landlord failed to repair a culvert on neighbouring land and as a result water escaped from the culvert and physically damaged the tenants property.(Perera v Vandiyar (1953) 1 WLR 672.

There are other instances of interference with quiet enjoyment. In Kenny v Pren 91963 1 QB (499) a landlord sent threatening letters and banged on the door of the tenant in addition to shouting physical abuse. This was also held to be a breach of quiet enjoyment. Basically, intimidation is seen to be a breach of the right to quiet enjoyment.

Whether substantial interference has taken place is a question of fact depending on the individual circumstance of the case. Acts which cause inconvenience to tenants but which do not actually disturb their enjoyment will not amount to a breach. For example where the landlord made a noise which merely inconvenienced the tenants privacy (Kelly v Battershell (1949) 2 All ER 830 CA).

Classes of people for whom the landlord is responsible

Acts by the landlord or by the landlords agents or servants or the tenants on the property. The landlord will not be responsible for unlawful acts of persons claiming title under the landlord, for example the tenants. Neither will the landlord be responsible for an act of disturbance by a third party or for a person who has superior title to the landlord, i.e. a head landlord.

Remedies for breach of covenant for quiet enjoyment

An action for breach of covenant for quiet enjoyment is an action for breach of contract and damages will normally be calculated on contractual principles. Contractual damages are usually limited to losses resulting from the breach. A tenant can therefore usually recover damages for inconvenience, for damage to his or her property and the costs of court proceedings.

A covenant to repair

Historically, repairing obligations have been confused and problematic. The basic principle being that in the absence of any covenants to repair then neither party has responsibility. The old principle of caveat emptor will apply, which means buyer beware. The usual situation that arises is that, where there is a written tenancy agreement there will usually be express covenants to repair within the agreement. Also, Landlord and Tenant law places an obligation on landlords to repair and there is a whole raft of case law where landlords have failed to comply with this. The main Act is the Landlord and Tenant Act 1985, section 11 which deals with repairing obligations. In addition to this Act there are other laws, e.g. Gas and Electrical safety which impose a burden upon a landlord.

Usually, the covenant to repair will be constructed in such a way that the landlord will be responsible for the structure and exterior and the tenant for the interior of the demise. In long leases, the landlord will raise monies through service charges either before works (sinking funds) or after works are complete. The 1985 Housing Act as amended by the Commonhold and Leasehold Reform Act 2002 imposes strict obligations on landlords in respect of service charges. The issue of repairing obligations will be discussed at greater length in the next chapter.

A covenant to insure
As it is in the interests of both parties to ensure that a property is safeguarded against fire or other disaster, then there will be an express covenant to insure in a lease. In short leases this is less common because of the short-term interest on the part of the tenant. However, in long leases the landlord will usually covenant to insure the premises with the costs passed on to the leaseholder. A usual problem that arises in this case is where the leaseholder feels that the costs of insurance are excessive. The courts usually uphold the landlords right to insure effectively as opposed to ensuring that the leaseholder receives value for money. However, powers contained within the landlord and tenant Acts and latterly the leasehold and Commonhold Reform Act 2002 give leaseholders a certain amount of rights when insurance is an issue.

The leaseholder may covenant to insure the premises at their own expense. The landlord may require the leaseholder to insure with a specific company or with a company approved by the landlord. If the covenant states that the landlord must approve the company then the landlord can refuse a company without giving reason (Viscount Tredegar v Harwood (1929) AC 72 HL).

If either the landlord or tenant voluntarily takes out insurance where there is no covenant to do so then there is no obligation to spend the insurance money on reinstating a building. Express covenants to insure normally cover this eventuality and expressly state that monies must be spent on reinstating the building. If the landlord has covenanted with the tenant to insure the building and premiums are collected then, in the absence of an express

15

undertaking to reinstate the building the courts will imply such a term as the insurance was intended to benefit both parties, not only the landlord (Mumford Hotels Ltd v Wheler (1964) Ch 177 (1963) 3 ALL ER 250).

Option to renew lease or purchase landlords interest

Options are different to restrictive covenants in that they give the tenant the right to do something in the future. There are three common rights which the tenant may acquire by way of option:

- An option to renew
- The right to end a tenancy
- The right to purchase the landlords interest in the property

These options will usually take the form of a covenant where the landlord will promise to perform the content of the covenant.

Option to renew

A landlord can, at the start of a fixed term tenancy, choose to give an option to renew the agreement for a further term. This is more common in periodic tenancies than long leases. Long leases are governed by Acts outside of the lease which give leaseholders a body of rights. The right to extend will almost always be with a qualification and this is that the tenant has maintained a well-managed tenancy. A requirement that there be no breach of covenant at the time of the exercise of the option will usually be strictly enforced.

One such example is where a tenant had failed to observe a covenant to repair at regular intervals (West Country Cleaners (Falmouth) Ltd v Saly (1966) 3 ALL ER 210 1 WLR 1485 CA). However, if the breach is not current at the point in time when the tenant wishes to exercise the option the tenant will not be prevented from exercising the right. One court case which highlights this is Bass Holdings Ltd v Morton Music Ltd (1987) 2 ALL ER 1001 CA where the landlord had, in the past, tried to forfeit the lease due to breach of covenant. The court had granted relief and the tenant had complied with all the conditions of relief.

In the same year following the breaches the tenant tried to exercise an option to renew. The courts held that, as the breaches were spent the tenant had the right to renew.

Option to determine

An option to end the tenancy (break clause) will usually exist in all tenancies and applies to both parties. The party who wishes to end the tenancy will have to comply strictly with the terms set out in the tenancy.

Option to purchase

An option to purchase gives the tenant the right to buy the landlords interest in the premises at a point in the future. An option to purchase is not regarded as part of a lease but runs collateral to the lease. This option will not usually be expressed in long residential leases but is more common in business leases.

b) Tenants covenants

1) a covenant to pay rent
2) a covenant to pay taxes
3) Various covenants regarding user
4) A covenant prohibiting assignment and/or subletting.

Covenant to pay rent

Although this particular covenant will be either an express or implied covenant, as the relationship between landlord and tenant is almost always for a consideration, the covenant will usually always be express. The amount of rent payable, and the time and method of payments are normally set out in the section of the lease called the 'reddendum'. The reddendum is followed by a list of the tenant's covenants, the first of which is normally a covenant to pay the rent reserved in the redendum. With long residential leases, the rent will usually consist of a ground rent, which will range from a peppercorn, to quite a substantial annual amount. In addition to rent, residential leaseholders will normally pay a maintenance charge (service charge). Service charges do not count as rent and are quite separate. In periodic tenancies, the rent will be higher, a market rent.

Rent review clauses

Leases, in particular tenancies and commercial tenancies will contain a rent review clause which will be effected at a certain point in time. Many commercial leases will specify 5 yearly intervals. The landlord will usually trigger this clause by the serving of a notice. The tenant must then respond within a certain time. Where a rent review clause has provided a timetable by which a landlord should begin the process, problems have arisen where the landlord has missed the due dates. The question that has arisen is whether or not the landlord loses the right to increase the rent after missing the dates laid out in the lease. Basically, the question is 'is time of the essence'? In United Scientific Holdings v Burnley Borough Council (1978) AC 904 (1977) 2 ALL ER 62, the House of Lords overruled earlier authority and held that the general presumption was that time was not of the essence. Time would be held to be of the essence only if:

a) the terms of the lease expressly provide that time should be of the essence
b) the terms of the lease indicate that time is to be of the essence where the rent review clause is linked to a clause providing an option and that option must be taken up within strict time limits
c) the surrounding circumstances indicate that time should be of the essence.

Certainty of rent

The rent expressed to be payable must be either certain or capable of being calculate with certainty at the date when payment is due. Rent is not always expressed in monetary terms, sometimes t is expressed in terms of services due in kind or in chattels. Courts always look favourably at leases where the rent is expressed as a certainty. However, the intention of the parties is the most important.

An option to renew a lease 'at a rent to be fixed at a price to be determined having regard to the market valuation of the premises at the time of exercising the option' has been held to be sufficiently certain (Brown v Gould (1972) Ch52 (1971) 2 All ER 1505). It can also be sufficient if the parties set out some machinery by means of which the rent can be determined, for example that it should be set by a person nominated by the Royal Institute of Chartered Surveyors. If the machinery set out in the agreement is not clarified or clear, the court may set its own mechanism for setting the rent (Sudbrooke Trading Estate Ltd v Eggleton (1983) 1 AC 444 (1982) 2 All ER 1). However, an option to renew a tenancy which stated that the new tenancy should be 'at a rent as may be agreed between parties in writing' and failed to provide any formula by which the rent could be calculated would not be sufficiently certain (Kings Motors (Oxford) Ltd v Lax (1970) 1 WLR 426).

The tenants covenants for rent should also state the date when the rent is payable. If rent is not paid by midnight on that day then it is held to be in arrears (Dibble v Bowater (1853) 2 E&B 564). Rent may be paid to the landlord or the landlord's agent. If the lease does not specify when the rent is due it becomes payable at the end of each period by which the rent has been calculated. In the case of a weekly tenancy it becomes payable at the end of each week but in the case of a term of years it becomes payable at the end of the year.

New requirements for the payment of ground rent have been introduced by the Commonhold and Leasehold Reform Act 2002. A notice separately demanding ground rent has to be issued. The rent will not be payable until such a notice has been served stating the amount and the date for payment.

In the case of weekly tenancies the tenant can set off rent against any landlords liabilities and this is held to be a defence against cases for possession on the grounds of rent arrears.

A covenant to pay taxes

The general rule here is that the tenant pays all taxes due in respect of the occupation. The situation is governed by statute in the case of council tax which is imposed on a person rather than a property (The Local Government Finance Act 1992). In the absence of an express covenant to the contrary it is generally assumed that the tenant is responsible for all taxes.

Covenants regarding user

The general rule at common law is that the tenant may use the premises for any lawful purpose. the doctrine of waste (see next chapter) will prevent the tenant from actively damaging the premises. If the landlord wishes to restrict use or retain any control over the premises then express provisions must be inserted in the lease. Any covenant prohibiting a particular type of user can be absolute or qualified.

Nuisance, damage or annoyance

Many leases will have a variety of different provisions restricting the tenant from committing certain acts. The covenant will be general and will cover any act of nuisance or annoyance committed on the premises. Many periodic tenancies used by local authorities or housing associations will have well worked out clauses whereas longer leases are usually more sparing. Nevertheless it is up to the courts to determine whether or not a nuisance has occurred.

Business use

Covenants may also seek to restrict the use to which the premises are put. Most residential leases will contain a covenant which will prohibit any form of business use. In such cases even partial business use will be a breach of covenant. However, in each case it will be a question of fact as to whether activities constitute business use. A tenant who takes in lodgers on a commercial basis would be in breach of covenant but not a tenant who takes in a lodger who lives with the family as part of that family (Segal Securities Ltd v Thoseby (1963) 1 ALL ER 500 (1963) 1 QB 887).

We will be discussing business tenancies further on in the book.

Covenant restricting assignment or sub-letting

In most tenancies there will be an express covenant which seeks to restrict the right to sublet or assign the lease. This effectively prevents the tenant from handing over the lease to another party. The wording of a covenant in the case of sub-letting or assignment is very important. For example a covenant' not to assign' is not breached if a tenant sublets (Russell v Beecham (1924) 1 KB 525 CA). A covenant not to sub let a premises does not restrict a tenant from sub letting part of the premises (Cook v Shoesmith (1951) 1 KB 752). In an attempt to cover all possibilities a landlord will usually draft a covenant requiring the tenant not to ' assign, sub-let or part with possession of the demised premises or any part thereof'. Even this wording might not be adequate if the tenant allows others to use the premises if the tenant is not excluded from the premises. Whether the tenant has or has not given up possession will be a question of fact. Covenants seeking to restrict assigning or sub letting will not prevent a tenant from taking in a lodger.

Absolute and qualified covenants

A covenant against assigning or subletting can be drafted in one of three ways:

1) an absolute covenant against assigning or subletting
2) a covenant prohibiting subletting or assigning without permission of the landlord
3) a covenant not to assign or sublet without landlords consent and that consent not to be unreasonably withheld.

Implied obligations in a lease

Not all obligations in a lease arise directly from express promises made between the landlord and tenant. Covenants can be implied by the common law, which although not expressly set out in the lease are nevertheless implied by common law. These covenants provide the basic minimum of protection for landlord and tenant where the lease fails to cover basic obligations. Implied covenants include:

Landlord's covenants:
   a) a covenant for quiet enjoyment

b) a covenant not to derogate from grant
c) an implied contractual duty of care to keep the common parts in good repair and order.

Tenants covenants

a) a covenant to pay rents
b) a covenant to pay taxes
c) not to assign or sub-let
d) a covenant to allow the landlord entry
e) a covenant not to deny the landlords title
f) a covenant to use the premises in a tenant like manner.

The above are implied in a lease even if not expressly stated.
Covenants implied by statute.
These are the covenants which, although not expressly set out in the agreement will be implied by statute to be part of that contractual agreement. They will augment the minimum standard of protection afforded by the common law.

Obligations arising in tort
These are the obligations based on the principle of a duty of care existing between the parties. These obligations arise independently of contract and so it is not strictly necessary for the parties involved to be in a relationship of landlord and tenant. Tortious obligations can arise either at common law of negligence or nuisance or for breach of a statutory duty.

Usual covenants
These are a particular class of covenants that are implied by the common law into a contract for a lease Where the parties to a lease fail to specify what terms the actual lease should contain, a term will be implied into the contract for the lease that the actual lease when it is granted will contain the ' usual covenants'.

Whether a covenant is a usual covenant or not is a question of fact and may vary depending on the nature of the premises, the purpose of letting and local conveyancing customs. (Flexman v

Corbett) 1930 1 Ch 672. However, certain basic covenants will be implied in every case:

Landlord's covenants

a) to allow the tenant quiet enjoyment
b) not to derogate from grant
c) a right of re-entry for non payment of rent
d) repairing obligations

Tenants covenants

a) to pay rent
b) to pay taxes
c) not to assign or sub-let
d) to keep and deliver up the premises in repair
e) to allow the landlord access to view and carry out repairs if the landlord has expressly covenanted to repair
f) not to deny the landlord title.

We can see that the usual covenants are in any case usually express covenants or implied.

3

Repairs

The area of Landlord and tenant law which causes the most contention is that of repairing obligations. Over the years the law regarding repairing responsibilities has tightened up to a degree where any covenants expressed in a lease are superseded by statute.

Caveat emptor
The old doctrine of caveat emptor is still relevant in that, certainly, a buyer should be aware of what he or she is buying. If a person buys a property in bad condition it is certainly going to be expensive to repair. Right at the outset, an in depth survey can save a lot of headaches.

Express agreement to repair
Where a written agreement exists there will, almost certainly, be an express covenant to repair. Parties are free to allocate the responsibility for repairs between them, in a way that they choose. In most cases now the responsibility is split, and is in accordance with the Landlord and Tenant Act 1985 s11. This states that the landlord shall be responsible for the structure and exterior and the tenant shall be responsible for the interior. The length of the lease will be a governing factor. Short term residential tenancies, fixed or periodic, will usually see the landlord responsible for and paying for the exterior and structure and, in most cases, interior repairs too, with some exceptions which we will list later. With a longer lease the landlord will exercise responsibility for the structure and exterior, in order to protect the reversion but the leaseholder will pay for these repairs by the way of service charges (see later).

Construction of repairing covenants

There are a number of ways of expressing a repairing covenant in a lease, depending on what the landlord wants to achieve from a letting. The following are the most common:

To put in repair

This is used where a premises are in disrepair at the outset of the lease and the leaseholder is obligated to bring the building up to a certain standard.

To leave in good repair

This can be expressed in a number of ways, such as to deliver, or yield up, in good repair. This expression is most commonly used and simply means to give the property back to the landlord in good repair, usually in the state that it was in at the commencement of the tenancy.

To keep in good condition

This goes beyond the normal covenant to keep in good repair or that it is imposing an obligation to keep the property in a good condition. Therefore, if a tenant allows a condition to continue, such as dampness and condensation, (Welsh v Greenwich LBC (2000) 49 EG 118 CA) then they are failing to keep the property in good condition.

To keep in repair

This is also a commonly used covenant and imposes an obligation on either tenant or landlord to ensure the premises are kept in good condition throughout the term.

To repair and renew

This is not so commonly used. In essence it does not impose any further obligations on a tenant other than to repair.

To carry out structural repairs

This covenant is usually to be found in longer leases where the burden to pay for repairs falls on the leaseholder.

Structural repairs means repairs to the fabric of the building such as roof, walls and foundations as opposed to repairs to decorations and other cosmetic elements.

It is usually common for the landlord to carry out these repairs with the financial burden placed on the leaseholder. Under periodic tenancies the landlord is responsible for carrying out and paying for structural alterations.

Another repairing term in common use within leases is fair wear and tear excepted. This is a clause most commonly used in short leases. It excludes the tenant from liability to repair damage which occurs due to the natural process of aging. The scope of such a clause is, of necessity, limited and would be limited to the following situations:

If the condition of the premises is abused by use which was not envisaged originally (Bonded Warehouse Co v Carr (1880) 5 CPD 507. If the damage is caused by extraordinary natural events such as earthquakes or floods. Where the cause of the damage can be traced back to a defect which was originally due to fair wear and tear but a consequence of this fair wear and tear has created a situation where the tenant would be responsible for the ensuing repair.

Liability for repairs

An obligation to repair will arise when there is disrepair and the party under an obligation to repair has notification of the defect. For a condition of disrepair to exist two factors must be present:

1) There must be some deterioration of the premises from a previous better condition.
2) The Party responsible must be under an express or implied obligation to repair that part that has deteriorated.

Disrepair cannot be equated with damage. If a house falls into disrepair because, for example, a roof has been leaking into the property then, if no one is covenanted to repair the roof then there is no disrepair. However, one main problem that has arisen here is to do with condensation. Condensation as a form of dampness is distinct from penetrating damp or rising damp. Condensation is usually generated by the occupants, through inadequate heating or ventilation. Water vapour which has been generated through kitchen or bathroom use, or by natural condensation from the human body, condenses on a cold surface and over time will cause damage to the property.

The most striking example of this problem was highlighted in Quick v Taff Ely BC (1985) 3 WLR 98). Severe condensation was caused largely by big metal frame windows. The dampness caused by the condensation caused damage to the tenants furniture, bedding, clothing and decorations. The court agreed that the dampness caused by the condensation made the living conditions of the tenant unbearable but held that the tenant had no remedy against the landlord. The landlord was covenanted to repair only the structure and exterior of the premises. The condensation had caused no damage to structure and exterior.

This finding can be compared to Staves and Staves v Leeds City Council (1992) 29 EG 119 CA) Damp and condensation caused small parts of plaster to perish and the tenant was held able to recover as the structure of the property had been damaged.

Condensation

Condensation dampness is a very significant part of disrepair and has been a source of distress and annoyance for many people. Two further cases highlight the ongoing problem of condensation cases. In Southwark LBC v McIntosh. (2002) 1 EGLR 25 it was held that there is no dispute when a property suffers from damp unless the damp arises from disrepair to the structure and the exterior of the dwelling itself or where the damp has caused damage to the structure or exterior.

In Lee v Leeds City Council (2003) 34 HLR 367 CA the court of appeal affirmed this view. The court, however, also decided that very serious levels of disrepair in a property let by a local authority, caused by condensation, might constitute a breach of the Human Rights Act, right to family and private life under article 8.

Notice of repair

No liability can arise for repair unless a landlord has been notified, either by the tenant or by the landlord's agent or by any other person. To establish liability the tenant must prove that the landlord had advance notification of the problem. The information given to a landlord must be sufficient to have enabled the landlord to take action (O'Brien v Robinson) (1973) AC 912). The complaints must relate to specific items of disrepair

The meaning of 'repair'

One case helped defined the meaning of a repair. In Calthorpe v McOscar (1924) 1 KB 176 CA repair was defined as ' making good damage so as to leave the subject as far as possible as though it had not been damaged.' However, it is really never possible to repair a building and leave it as new.

To repair or renew

When a tenant is granted a lease, particularly a lease of an older property, obviously the components of the house will have aged. If one of the components becomes defective and is replaced with a new component this is renewal. All repair involves renewal and ongoing renewal of components over time will be classed as repair even if the whole building is renewed over time (Luncott v Wakeley and Wheeler (1911) 1KB 905).

The other side of this coin is if a house is deemed to be in such a bad condition that the only course is renewal of the whole. This is clearly not repair. In between, there are many situations where courts have to make decisions between repair and renewal. Each case is considered on its own merit and there is a host of case law considering the distinction.

Inherent defects

As we have seen, basically repair means making good damage to a part of the property. Situations arise however, where inherent defects arise. It is argued that the obligations to repair do not arise when the defect arises from inherent defects in the design or construction of the building. Certain cases have highlighted and supported this view. In Collins v Flynn (1963) 2 ALL ER 1068 a building, due to inadequate foundations collapsed as a result of a structure supporting part of the back and sidewall of a house. It was held that to replace the foundations and replace the structure amounted to an improvement and not a repair.

The doctrine of inherent defect was firmly laid out in Ravenseft Ltd v Davstone Ltd (1980) 1QB 12. Here, stone cladding had become detached from a building due to failure to install expansion joints. The judge in that case found that this was an inherent defect but could be remedied as a repair as the cost of doing so was relatively small. Two other cases highlight the differences between inherent defect and a repair. In Elmcroft Developments Ltd v Tankersley Sawyer (1984) 270 Eg 1289, the original slate damp course in a block of flats had been installed too low, with the result that the lower flats subject to the damp course were damp. To remedy the damp it was necessary to install a new silicone damp course. The courts held that this was repair. The other case, Eyre v McCraken (2000) 80 P&CR 220 CA held that as there was no damp proof course in the building concerned then this was an inherent defect.

Standards of repair

The main case highlighting standards of repairs was that of Proudfoot v Hart (1890) 25 QBD 42. In that case, the judge stated:

'good tenantable repair is such a repair that, having regard to the age, character and locality of the house, would make it reasonably fit for the occupation of a reasonably minded tenant of the class who would be likely to take it'.

Therefore, age, character and location are key factors. Differing properties require different standards, as do differing tenants.

However, over the years various cases have challenged this doctrine as being too rigid. One view which has arisen is that the standard of repair is determined at the beginning rather than the end of the tenancy. Age would obviously be a factor as a tenant cannot possibly be expected to maintain a property as new because of the inevitable aging process.

Common law obligations on landlords

The common law imposes certain obligations to repair on a landlord, despite the general rule that in the absence of an express agreement there is no obligation to repair.

Implied standards of fitness for human habitation at commencement of a tenancy of furnished premises.

In the case of furnished premises the common law will imply an obligation to ensure that at the start of a tenancy the premises are fit for human obligation. This was established in Smith v Marrable (1843) 11 MW 5. This established a common law principle which has been superseded by legislation, primarily the Housing Act 1985 as amended by the Local Government and Housing Act 1989. These Acts are used as a guide when determining fitness for human habitation.

If the premises are not fit for human habitation then the tenant is entitled to quit and to recover damages.

Common parts

Common parts and their upkeep and repair have historically presented a problem to landlords and tenant. There are usually common parts, particularly in large blocks of flats that the tenants have the right to use, but which are separate to the premises leased to the tenant. There may be lifts, staircases, rubbish chutes and so on. Usually, the responsibility for upkeep of the common parts will fall on the landlord with the cost recovered through a service charge. However, sometimes there is no express agreement allocated to maintenance of common parts.

If the tenancy was granted after 15th January 1989 then there is an implied term in an agreement that the landlord has an obligation to repair and maintain common parts. This includes cleanliness and security. This implied obligation is in the 1988 Housing Act s 11(a) as supplemented by the HA 1988 s 116(1). For tenancies granted before this date then there may be a contractual duty of care implied into the contract. In Liverpool City Council v Irwin (1977) AC 239 (1976) ALL ER 39 the tenants of a 15 storey high-rise block rented from the council. There was no proper tenancy agreement only a document entitled 'conditions of tenancy'. This document did not refer to any of the council's obligations. The lifts were out of order due to vandalism and the staircases were poorly lit and also vandalised. The courts considered the situation, specifically the conditions of tenancy. It concluded that, as a matter of necessity a contractual obligation had to be implied into the contract. This imposed a duty of care upon the landlord to maintain common parts.

The contractual duty of care is implied only in certain circumstances. It applies only to the common areas of a building which are within a landlord's control. The term is implied only in circumstances where not to repair would render the contract futile. It is not an absolute duty of care. The landlord need only take a reasonable duty of care. The duty of care only applied to the parties to the contract.

As the common parts are within the landlords control a tenant, or anyone else, does not need to give a landlord notice of repair.

Common law obligations on tenants

In common law a tenant is under a duty to look after a premises in a 'tenant like manner'. This doctrine was laid out by Lord Denning in the case of Warren v keen (1953) 2 ALL ER 1118 at 1121 (1954) QB 15 at 20. In this case, Lord Denning stated:

'The tenant must take proper care of the place, he must, if he is going away for the winter, turn off the water and empty the boiler. he must clean the chimneys, if necessary, and also the windows. He must mend the electric light when it fuses. He must unstop the sink when blocked by his waste. In short, he must do the little jobs around the place that a reasonable tenant would do. In addition, he must, of course, not damage the house, wilfully or negligently and he must see that his family and guests do not damage it. If they do, he must repair it'.

31

However, Lord Denning also said that ' if the house falls into disrepair through fair wear and tear or through lapse of time, or for any reason not caused by him, the tenant is not liable to repair it'.

Obligation not to commit waste

To commit waste means doing, or failing to do, any act which changes or alters the land. There is voluntary waste where the tenant causes damage to the premises and permissive waste where the premises falls into disrepair because the tenant fails to take action to prevent deterioration.

The extent of the implied obligations imposed on the tenant will vary with the length of the lease. A fixed term lease is liable for both voluntary and permissive waste. A yearly tenant is liable for only voluntary waste with the additional obligation that he or she should keep the premises wind and watertight. However, a yearly tenancy will not be liable for fair wear and tear. A tenant with a shorter periodic tenancy will be liable for only voluntary waste.

Obligation to allow the landlord entry to inspect and repair

This is an implied obligation in the absence of any express agreement.

Covenants implied by statute

In the Landlord and Tenant Act 1985 s 8(1) there are two provisions relating to houses on a low rent and houses on a short lease. On a low rent, there is implied on the part of the landlord:

1) a condition that, at the commencement of the tenancy the premises are fit for human habitation.
2) An undertaking that, during the course of the tenancy the premises will be kept in all respects fit for human habitation.

These terms are implied regardless of any express obligations to the contrary. If the premises are let for more than three years and there is a term placing an obligation upon the tenant to keep in habitable condition s 8 will not apply. 'House' includes flats and bed sits and a tenancy includes all sub tenancies but not a licence. The rent levels in this provision are set so low that the section is now largely irrelevant.

For the majority of tenants on a short tenancy, week-by-week or short fixed term, The landlord and Tenant Act 1985 s (11) will be the repairing covenant. Section 11 applies to any lease of a dwelling house granted after 24th October 1961 for a term of less than seven years. Section 11 does not apply to business tenancies, to tenancies of agricultural holdings or to tenancies granted after 3rd October 1980 by local authorities or to tenancies granted after 3rd October 1980 by the Crown.

The LTA 1985 s 11 states:

1) in a lease to which this section applies...there is implied a covenant by the lessor-

    a) to keep in repair the structure and exterior of the dwelling house (including drains, gutters and external pipes)

    b) to keep in repair and proper working order the installations in the dwelling house for the supply of gas, water, and electricity and for sanitation including basins sinks baths and sanitary conveniences, but not other fixtures and fittings and appliances for making use of gas, water or electricity and:

    c) to keep in repair and proper working order the installations in the dwelling house for space heating and heating water.

Section 11 does not impose a duty on a landlord:

a) to carry out works or repairs for which the lessee is liable by virtue of his duty to use the premises in a tenant like manner. S (11) (2) (a). Thus the tenant will still be responsible for performing minor everyday repairs about the house.

b) To rebuild or reinstate the premises in case of destruction or damage by fire, or by tempest or flood or other inevitable accident s (11) (2) (b).

c) To keep in repair or maintain anything which the lessee is entitled to remove from the dwelling house.

Structure and exterior

Over the years a great body of case law has built up regarding the meaning of structure and exterior of a dwelling. 'Structure' in Irvine v Moran (1991) 1 EGLR 261, was held not to include the entire dwelling house but only those elements that gave it its essential appearance, stability and shape. It is important to note that implied covenants only extend to the structure and exterior of the dwelling house concerned, i.e. a third floor flat, and not the whole building although for tenancies granted after 15th January 1989 a new section was introduced into the 1985 HA, s 11(1A) which extended this obligation to the whole of a building in which a lessor has an interest.

Windows are regarded as part of the exterior (Ball and Plummer (1879) 2 TLR 887 CA) and elements such as plasterwork are regarded as part of the structure.

Installations

Section 11 also covers installations for the supply of gas, water and electricity and sanitation and also installations for space heating and heating water. The obligation to keep installations in proper working order may also include remedying design faults that cause subsequent problems of use. For example in Liverpool City Council v Irwin (1977) AC 239 a landlord was obliged to replace cisterns which caused lavatories to overflow. The problem was caused by design. Again, where s 11 did not cover any areas other than a tenants flat, for all tenancies granted after 15th January 1989 the landlord is placed under an obligation to keep in repair and proper working order an installation which serves a dwelling house and either forms any part of the building in which the lessor has an interest or is owned by the lessor and is under his control.

Remedies against a tenant for non-repair

If a landlord has expressly reserved a right of re-entry in a lease or tenancy agreement he may be able to forfeit the lease in the event of disrepair. However, this remedy is now almost impossible under a long lease. It is much easier to achieve under a periodic tenancy. In the case of leases of seven years or more then the landlord also has to comply with the provisions of s 1 of the Leasehold Property (Repairs) Act 1938, of more which below.

Damages

A landlord can seek damages from a court for disrepair which are usually equal to the diminution of the value of the property owing to the disrepair. If a lease of a property has many years to run then the amount recoverable will be less. Therefore the amount of damages recoverable will depend on the un-expired term.

If a landlord brings an action for damages after a tenancy has ended then the amount of damages will depend on the extent of the cost of carrying out the repairs to the property. In this case, the landlord would sue on the basis of the covenant to leave in repair rather than to keep in repair.

Section 18 of the Landlord and Tenant Act 1927 provides the framework for the amount of damages payable to a tenant. It states that damages will not exceed the value of the diminution of the market value of the property due to disrepair. If the market is high at the time then it is possible that the landlord may not be able to recover any money.

Long leases

The Leasehold Property (Repairs) Act 1938 imposes special restrictions upon a landlord. The Act applies to a long lease over seven years and the aim of the Act is to protect a leaseholder against forfeiture mid term because of failure to carry out repairs that may be difficult to remedy.

If a landlord wishes to take action then the Act contains a strict notice procedure, on both sides which has to be observed. The tenant, on receipt of a notice from a landlord, can serve a counter notice and the landlord, if he or she wants to further the action, must prove the following:

1) that the value of the reversion has been substantially diminished by the breach or that the breach must be immediately remedied to prevent the value being diminished.
2) That the breach must be immediately remedied to comply with a by-law, an Act of Parliament, a court order or a requirement of a local authority.
3) That if the tenant is not in occupation of the whole premises the breach must be immediately remedied in the interests of the occupier of the premises or part of the premises.
4) That the breach can be immediately remedied at relatively small expense in comparison with the probable cost of the work is left un-remedied.
5) That there are special circumstances which in the courts opinion are just and equitable to grant leave.

Entering a property to carry out repairs

Where the landlord is under an obligation to repair a property then there will be an implied right to enter. Usually, this is directly expressed in a lease. This provision will also enable the landlord to recover the costs of the work due. This was expressed in the case of Jervis v Harris (1996) 1 ALL ER 303. The amount recoverable is not restricted by section 18 of the LTA 1927.

It is obvious that, when deciding to enter a property, the provisions of the lease must be adhered to. Leases will have a clause, usually, to allow landlords access in emergency if the disrepair is considered such that it is either life threatening or threatening immediate significant damage to the property. If this is the case, and can be demonstrated as such then the landlord is within his or her rights to force entry. In all other cases, reasonable notice must be given and every attempt made to remedy the repair, on the tenant's part, before gaining entry.

Tenants remedies against a non-repairing landlord

The aim of damages in this case is to restore the tenant to a position where they would have been before the problem of disrepair. The damages can be recovered whether the covenant is express or implied. The landlord will only be liable for damages if they have been informed of the disrepair. A reasonable period must be allowed for the landlord to remedy the disrepair. If the tenant refuses to give the landlord access to carry out the repairs then no damages are recoverable (Granada Theatres Ltd v Freehold Investment (Leytonstone) Ltd 1959 Ch 529 (1959) 2 ALL ER 176). The circumstances of the case will determine the damages awarded.

Where a landlord is in breach of repairing covenants the tenant may carry out repairs and then deduct the cost of the repairs from future rent (Lee Parker v Izzet (1971) 3 ALL ER 1099 (1971). Before taking this action the tenant must make sure that the landlord has been notified of the repair and that the repair falls within the scope of the landlords obligations. Withholding of rent on these grounds can be used in a counter-claim for rent arrears.

There are other remedies for disrepair, such as taking out an interim injunction against a landlord, requiring the landlord to do the works. This however, can be costly. It has to be achieved through the Civil Procedure Rules parts 23 and 25 and will usually entail the tenant obtaining a surveyors report. It is only usual to obtain an injunction if the disrepair is significant and it is also threatening the property or the occupants.

Courts may order specific performance of a covenant to repair. A residential tenant may obtain an order requiring specific performance compelling a landlord to fulfil his or her duty.

Appointment of a receiver and appointment of a manager

If a landlord has neglected his duties for years and the tenant sees no point in pursuing the landlord then an application can be made to a court for a receiver to take over the management of the property. The courts will not appoint a receiver to take over management of local authority housing (Parker v Camden Council (1986) CH 162 (1985) 2 ALL ER 141 CA).

Under PT 2 of the Landlord and Tenant Act 1987, as amended by the Housing Act 1996 ss 85 and 86 the tenant may apply to the Leasehold Valuation Tribunal for the appointment of a manager where a landlord persistently fails to maintain a block consisting of two or more flats, Once a notice has been served on a landlord informing him or her of the disrepair and neglect and the landlord has ignored the notice then an application can be made. These provisions do not apply if the landlord is a local authority, resident landlord or the tenant is a business tenant.

Repair notices

Local housing authorities have wide powers over the condition of local housing. These powers are contained within the Housing Act 1985 as supplemented by the Local Government and Housing Act 1989. Notices can be served for a variety of purposes. In addition Environmental Health Departments have significant powers under the Environmental Protection Act 1990.

Negligence and repair

Liability for negligence is based on a duty of care. The duty of care is central to many acts, and, in the case of disrepair if a person or persons, or other entity, fails to take reasonable care through some act or omission and the result is that the other person suffers injury or damage, the injured party can recover damage.

As with other areas of landlord and tenant, the principle of caveat emptor applies. This was illustrated in Robbins v Jones (1863) 15 CB 9NS) 221 at 430:

A landlord who lets a house in a dangerous state is not liable to the tenants customers or guests for accidents happening during the term: for fraud apart, there is no law against letting a tumble down house, and the tenants remedy is upon his contract, if any.

However, society has, thankfully, moved on since then. There are now laws which ensure that a landlord has to maintain a property in good condition.

When is a landlord liable for negligence?

In recent years the law of negligence has expanded to cover all of those involved in the design and construction of the building.

The duty of care extends to common parts also for the acts of third parties. In King v Liverpool city council 91986) 1 WLR 890 the tenant lived in a block of flats owned by the council. A flat above became vacant. The tenant requested that the council secure this flat which it failed to do and it was vandalised and also water flooded out the flat below. The landlord was held liable for the acts of these third parties.

Likewise the landlord is also responsible for any nuisance cause by neglect. Only a person in possession of a premises can sue in nuisance.

There are two main statutory provisions that place a duty of care on a landlord:

Occupiers Liability Act 1957

This provides that:

1) An occupier of a premises owes the same duty 'the common duty of care' to all visitors except in so far as he is free to and does extend, restrict, modify or exclude his duty to any visits or visitors by agreement or otherwise.

2) The common duty of care is a duty to take such care as in all the circumstances of the case is reasonable to se that the visitor will be reasonably safe in using the premises for the purposes for which he is invited or permitted by the occupier to be there.

3) The circumstances relevant for the present purpose include the degree of care, and of want of care, which would ordinarily be looked for in such a visitor so that (for example) in proper cases-

   a) an occupier must be prepared for children to be less careful than adults: and

   b) an occupier may expect that a person, in the exercise of his calling, will appreciate and guard against any special risks ordinarily incident to it, as far as the occupier leaves him free to do so.

The Defective Premises Act 1972

Section 1 of this act imposes a duty on a person or persons who undertake work for, in connection with, the provision of a dwelling:

a) to do the work in a professional or workmanlike manner
b) to use proper materials
c) to ensure with regard to that work that the dwelling will be ft for habitation when completed.

This again applies to all involved in the construction process. However, s 2 of the Act provides that s 1 will not apply to dwellings which are covered by an approved scheme of purchase protection such as NHBC. Section 1 is also restricted by the six year limitation period which begins to run when the building is completed and will only apply to work carried out after commencement of the Act (1 January 1974).

Section 3 of the Act applies to works carried out prior to a sale or letting. It imposes a duty of care in negligence upon anyone carrying out works of construction, repair, maintenance or demolition. The duty is owed to anyone who might reasonably be affected by the defects created and covers tenants, family visitors. The duty also continues to be owed if the property is sold or let.

Section 4 is the most important provision in the Act:
1)where the premises are let under a tenancy which puts on the landlord an obligation to the tenant for the maintenance or repair of the premises, the landlord owes to all persons who might reasonably be expected to be affected by defects in the state of the premises a duty to take such care as is reasonable in all circumstances to see that they are reasonably safe form personal injury or from damage to their property caused by a relevant defect.

The main thrust of lawyers when suing for disrepair hinges on this section. There have been shameful misuses of this section by 'ambulance chasing solicitors' attacking public sector landlords.

Nevertheless, it is the most effective provision on which to base a disrepair claim.

Knowledge of the defect

S2 of the Act provides:

2) the said duty is owed if the landlord knows whether as a result of being notified by the tenant or otherwise) or if he ought in all the circumstances to have known of the relevant defect.

The landlord does not have to have actual knowledge of the defect. In Clarke v Taff Ely BC (1984) 10 hLR 44, a tenant was injured when the floor collapsed The tenant had not informed the council of the state of the floor. However, the council was held to be liable for the defect. The house in question and the state of the floorboards should have been inspected.

4

Assignments

Assignments and continuing responsibilities

When one person enters into a tenancy with another a contractual relationship is created. Privity of contract is created, which means that the terms of the contract can be enforced against parties to the contract. However, tenancies can be passed on through assignment or another tenancy granted (sublet) which effectively passes on the contractual responsibility to another party. There are rules which determine what happens in these situations.

The Landlord and Tenant (Covenants) Act 1995 changed the rules regarding ongoing responsibilities when assigning or subletting. The Act does not act retrospectively which means that there are two sets of rules governing tenancies prior to the introduction of the 1995 Act, i.e. tenancies granted prior to January 1st 1996 and tenancies granted after that date.

Sub-letting a tenancy

To create a sub-lease the tenant, as we have seen, will grant a term less than the head lease. A sub-lease should normally be granted by deed unless it is granted for a period of less than three years.

Assignment

When a lease is assigned the tenant hands over his or her interest in the property entirely. The original tenant (assignor) retains no reversion and the new tenant (the assignee) takes over the position of the old tenant. However, in certain circumstances this does not mean that the outgoing person ceases to have any obligations.

To ensure that a legal estate is passed on all assignments must be made by deed (LPA 1925 s52(1)). This applies to leases whether created orally, in writing or by deed.

Some assignments are involuntary, such as assignment following death. If a tenant dies then the Administration of Estates Act will govern the vesting of the tenancy in another as part of an estate. Likewise, if bankruptcy occurs then the tenancy will vest in the trustee in bankruptcy.

Tenant's liability after sub-letting or assignment

When sub-letting or assignment occurs, a person who was not party to the original contract between landlord and tenant has acquired an interest in either part or whole of the property. The question here is to what extent is a person who was party to the original contract still bound by the covenants even though assignment or sub-letting has taken place? Also, to what extent is a person who has acquired an interest bound by the contract?

Under tenancies entered into before 1st January 1996, contractual liability does not end simply because the person who entered into the contract has handed over his interest to a third party. This is because a tenant who entered into a contract prior to 1st January 1996 will expressly covenant to be responsible for the acts and omissions of his successor in title and persons deriving title under the tenant (i.e. sub-tenants). Even in the absence of express terms to this effect they will be implied by s79 of the LPA 1925 unless they have been expressly excluded.

One example is that a party to the original contract will remain liable for the rent due by the new party to the contract for the term of the lease. A Case which highlights this is Estates Gazette v Benjamin Restaurants (1994) 26 EG 140 CA.

This situation can be seen as unjust and the 1995 Act came into being in order to remedy the problem. Under the old Act, the original tenant virtually guarantees the lease and it is up to the tenant to ensure that they pick responsible assignees. The 1995 Act, in addition to changing the position between assignor and landlord, has placed a time limit within which the landlord can pursue the tenant for breach of covenant under leases made prior to 1st January 1996, which is 6 months.

It was even thought that original tenants were liable for breaches of covenants which were variations of the lease made between the new tenant and the landlord. However, one case highlighted this as unjust *Friends Provident Life Office v British Railways Board* (1996) 1 ALL ER 336.

Statutory restrictions on the common law principles

Though the majority of the provisions in the 1995 Act apply to tenancies post- January 1st 1996 ss17-20 apply to old tenancies as well and offset the consequences of the common law for those who entered into tenancies prior to January 1st 1996:

a) Restriction on liability for rent and service charge. Section 17 imposes a procedure upon a landlord who wishes to recover money from a former tenant. It provides that a former tenant will not be liable to the landlord to pay any fixed charge including both rent and service charge, unless, within six months of that charge being due, the landlord services notice on the former tenant. Effectively, the notice provides a cut-off point after which the landlord cannot recover monies owed.

b) Restriction on liability where tenancy is subsequently varied. Section 18 is included in the 1995 Act where this situation exists It provides that a former tenant will not be liable to pay any amount in respect of a covenant that has been varied.

c) Overriding leases. Once a tenancy has been assigned the main problem encountered by a former tenant is his or her lack of control over subsequent assignees. The 1995 Act enables the original tenant faced with the prospect of being sued, to force the the landlord to grant him or her with an overriding lease. This restores some power to the former tenant by making him or her the assignees immediate landlord. However, an original tenant will only be able to demand an overriding lease where full payment of the original demand had been made to the landlord.

An original tenant who wishes to demand an overriding lease has to do so in writing within 12 months of the landlords demand for payment being made. The landlord has a liability to grant an overriding lease within a reasonable time. The original tenant will be liable for costs.

The new rules

If the tenancy is granted after 1st January 1996 the position is governed by statue as opposed to common law which governs tenancies granted prior to 1st Jan 1996. Section 5 of the 1995 Act gets rid of the principle of privity of contract. It provides that on assignment of the whole of the premises the tenant will be automatically released from the tenant covenants of the tenancy and will cease to be entitled to the landlords covenants of the tenancy from the date of assignment (s5(2)). If the tenant assigns only part of the premises demised to him or her then the automatic release will only apply to the extent that the covenants fail to be complied with in relation to that part of the demised premises. Where covenants are clearly related to a part of a building that has been demised the tenant will continue to be liable. Where they are not clearly related to a part then the assignor and assignee will be jointly liable.

Because of this new system of statutory release it is no longer necessary for a tenant to be deemed to covenant on behalf of himself his successors in title and the persons deriving title under him nor for an implied indemnity covenant to be inserted into the lease.

Authorised guarantee agreements

The 1995 Act has introduced a mechanism which goes some way towards protecting landlords as they now no longer have any say in selecting assignees after 1st Jan 1996. The authorised guarantee agreement requires in certain circumstances, that a tenant remains contractually liable after assignment. The landlord can require this in the following circumstances:

a) the agreement must be one under which the tenant guarantees the performance of the covenant by the assignee (s16(2) (a))
b) there must be a covenant against assignment in the lease which prevents the tenant from effecting the assignment without the consent of the landlord (s16 (3)(a):
c) the assignment of a lease is subject to a condition that requires the tenant to enter into an agreement guaranteeing the performance of the covenant by the assignee (s16(3)(c)

The scope of the authorised agreement is limited by statute. It must not impose on the tenant any requirement to guarantee in any way the performance of the relevant covenant by any other than the immediate assignee and it must not impose on the tenant any liability restriction or requirement of whatever nature in relation to any time after the assignee is released from that covenant by virtue of the 1995 Act. Thus the immediate tenant will be required to guarantee the immediate assignee.

Excluded assignments
The release of landlord and tenant covenants will not apply in the case of an excluded assignment. There are two types of excluded assignment:

a) assignments in breach of a covenant in a tenancy, for example where the agreement contains a covenant forbidding assignment;
b) assignments by operation of law such as death or bankruptcy.

Where a landlord or tenant remains bound because the assignment made was an excluded assignment he or she will nevertheless be released if and when a further assignment of the tenancy is made provided that the further assignment is not an excluded assignment.

Liability between persons not party to the original agreement

In relation to the person who acquires an interest in land, under the old rules the situation is governed by the rule in Spencers Case (1583) 5 Co Rep 16a. The rule states that the assignee of a tenancy will acquire both the burden and the benefits of the covenants in a lease provided that:

a) there is privity of estate between the person seeking to enforce the covenant and the person against whom he is seeking to enforce it;

b) the covenant in question touches and concerns the land.

Privity of estate

This arises when two parties are in a relationship of landlord and tenant. There will be privity of estate between parties regardless of whether the parties have contracted with each other.

Covenants that touch and concern the land

A covenant will 'touch and concern the land' if it affects landlord and tenant. One such case that highlighted this was Breams Property Investment Co Ltd v Stroulger (1948) 2 KB 1.

Virtually all of the common covenants considered so far in this book touch the land. Covenants concerning rent and repair, user and quiet enjoyment will certainly touch the land. Although the number of covenants can be unlimited the following covenants have been held to touch the land:

a) A covenant requiring the tenant to sell only a landlords brand of product on the premises Clegg v Hands (1890) 44 ChD 503.

b) A covenant requiring a tenant not to permit a particular person to be involved with the running of the business on the premises (Lewin v American and Colonial Distributors Ltd (1945) Ch 255 1 ALL ER 529.

A covenant will not touch the land if it does not concern the landlord and tenant in their capacity as landlord and tenant or of it does not directly reference the land. Such covenants have been held to be the option to buy the premises or an entitlement to put up advertising.

Liability after assignment under the new rules
For new tenancies, as we have seen, the situation is governed by statute. Section 3 of the 1995 Act provides:

(1) The benefit and burden of all landlord and tenant covenants of a tenancy-

a) shall be annexed and incident to the whole and to each and every part of the premises demised by the tenancy and the reversion in them, and
b) shall in accordance with this section pass on assignment of the whole or any part of the whole premises or the reversion in them.

Thus section 3 fixes the benefits and burdens of all covenants to the land. There is no need to consider whether the covenant in question touches and concerns the land. In addition, where a tenant assigns his or her tenancy the assignee will become bound by the tenants covenants in the tenancy and entitled to the benefits of the landlord covenants in the tenancy. The provisions contain a number of exceptions. First the assignee will not be bound by tenant covenants that immediately before the assignment did not bind the assignor.

Liability of the assignor to the assignee
Where an assignment was made before 1st July 1994 the Law of Property Act 1925 s76 implies a number of covenants into the transaction on the part of the assignor for the benefit of the assignee. These are: covenants for title; a covenant for quiet enjoyment; a covenant for further assurance and a covenant that the lease is not liable to forfeiture and that the tenants covenants have been performed by the assignor.

Where the assignment was made after July 1st 1994, Part 1 of the Law of Property Act (Miscellaneous Provisions) 1994 will apply to the transaction. Again, these provisions imply covenants on the part of the assignor that he or she has good title, and in the case of leasehold land that the lease is subsisting at the date of disposition and that there is no breach of the tenants obligation and that the lease is not liable to forfeiture.

Liability of the assignee to the assignor

Assignments made prior to the coming into force of the Landlord and Tenant (covenants) Act 1995 will contain an implied covenant on the part of the assignee that he or she would, at all times from the date of the assignment, pay the rent and perform the tenants covenants and indemnify the assignor against failure to do so. Where the assignment was made after 1st January 1996 the exclusion of continuing liability afforded to the tenant by the 1995 Act means that this implied covenant is no longer necessary.

Liability after the sale of the landlords interest in the property

In the case of tenancies entered into before 1st January 1996 the question as to whether the benefit and burden of the covenants in the original lease will run to bind an assignee of the reversion is determined by statute. Section 141 of the LPA 1925 states that 'the rent reserved by a lease and the benefits of all the covenants in a lease which refer to the subject matter in the lease' will run to benefit the assignee of the conversion. In addition the obligations will run to bind an assignee.

Liability after the sale of the reversion under the new rules

For new tenancies the rules which govern the transmission of the benefit and burden of the covenants contained in the original lease after the assignment of the reversion are almost identical to those which govern transmission when there is an assignment of the tenancy. An assignee of the landlords reversion will be bound by the landlords covenants in the tenancy and becomes entitled to the benefit of the tenants covenants.

Liability of sub-lessees

Under the old rules the relationship is between the landlord and the lessee in a contractual relationship of privity of contract. The sub-lessee is in a contractual relationship with the lessee. The covenants in a head tenancy will not run to bind a sub-lessee. There is one exception. A head lessee may be able to enforce a covenant in the head tenancy against a sub-lessee under the rule in Tulk v Moxhay (1848) 2 Ph 774. This rule allows the head landlord to enforce a restrictive covenant against any occupier who takes possession of the premises with notice of the covenant. A restrictive covenant can be registered as a minor interest in registered land or as a class D(ii) land charge in unregistered land. If the restrictive covenant is registered the occupier will be deemed to have notice of that covenant even if they have no knowledge of it.

Under the new rules

The provisions of the 1995 Act do not apply to the transmission of the burdens and benefits of covenants on assignment. They do not function to make covenants enforceable between a head landlord and a sub-tenant.

5

The Protected Tenant – The Rent Act 1977

If a tenancy agreement was granted before 15th January 1989 then, in most cases, it will be a Rent Act protected agreement. However, there are a number of exceptions to this and they are listed further on in this chapter.

Many tenancies nowadays are assured tenancies. However, despite this, there are a significant number of older Rent Act protected tenancies in existence.

What Rent Act protection means is that the rules which guide the conduct of the landlord and tenant are laid down in the 1977 Rent Act.

This Act was passed to give tenants more security in their home. It is called a Rent Act because its main purpose is to regulate rents, but the Act also gives tenants other rights such as protection from eviction.

It is mainly only tenants who can enjoy protection under the Rent Act of 1977, not usually licensees or trespassers who have limited rights. A tenancy will be protected provided that the landlord does not live on the premises. If a landlord lives in the same accommodation as the tenant then the tenant will not be protected by the 1977 Rent Act. To live in the same premises means to share the same flat as the tenant and not, for example, to live in the same block of flats.

In addition, Rent Act protection means that the rent will be regulated This basically means that the tenant has the right to a fair rent set by a Rent Officer employed by the local authority.

The fair rent is set every two years and the landlord is not free to charge as he or she wishes. Once set the rent cannot be altered.

Rent Act protection also means protection from eviction which means that the landlord is not free to evict.

For a tenancy to be protected, however, the tenant must be using the property as his/her main residence. If they are not, and the fact can be proved, then they will lose protection and the landlord can evict with less trouble.

SECURITY: THE WAYS IN WHICH THE TENANT CAN LOSE HIS/HER HOME AS A PROTECTED TENANT

When a tenant signs a tenancy agreement he or she is signing a contract where both landlord and tenant are agreeing to accept certain rights and responsibilities.

In the agreement, there are a number of grounds for possession which enable the landlord to recover his or her property if the contract is broken by the tenant, eg, by not paying the rent. These may not always be referred to in the agreement but this can be found in the 1977 Rent Act.

If a landlord wishes to take back his or her property he/she must serve the tenant with a notice to quit (the premises) which must give twenty eight days notice of intention to seek possession of the property (to begin to recover the property) and, following the expiry of the twenty eight days an application must be made to court to repossess the property.

When the landlord serves the notice to quit the reasons for his doing so should be stated in a covering letter to the tenant and should be based on the grounds for possession outlined in the agreement.

A landlord cannot simply evict a tenant, or use menaces (harassment) to do so. There is protection (Protection from Eviction Act 1977) and the landlord must apply to court to get a tenant out once the twenty eight days have expired.

When a landlord has served a notice to quit, a tenancy becomes a "statutory tenancy" which exists until a court order brings it to an end.

Briefly, the reasons for a landlord wanting possession will be based on one of ten mandatory or ten discretionary grounds for possession.

Mandatory grounds for possession means that the court must

give the landlord possession of the property, which means that the judge has no choice in the matter.

Discretionary grounds for possession means that the court can exercise some discretion in the matter (i.e. can decide whether or not to order eviction) and it is up to the landlord to prove that he is being reasonable. Discretionary grounds usually correspond to the tenants obligations in the tenancy.

It is very rare, in the first instance, if the grounds are discretionary, for a landlord to gain possession of a property unless it is obviously abandoned or the circumstances are so dramatic. Usually a suspended order will be granted.

A suspended order means that the tenant will be given a period of time within which to solve the problem, i.e come to an agreement with the landlord. This time period is, normally, twenty eight days. So, for example, if a tenant has broken an agreement to pay the rent, the judge may give twenty eight days in which either to pay the full amount or to reach an agreement with the landlord.

Listed below are the grounds for possession which can be used against a tenant by a landlord. Full details of all grounds can be found in the 1977 Rent Act

The discretionary grounds for possession of property covered by the 1977 Rent Act

Ground One is where the tenant has not paid his or her rent or has broken some other condition of the tenancy.

Ground One covers any other condition of the tenancy. This includes noise nuisance, unreasonable behaviour and, usually, racial or sexual harassment.

Ground Two is where the tenant is using the premises for immoral or illegal purposes, eg, selling drugs, prostitution. It also covers nuisance and annoyance to neighbours.

Grounds Three and Four are connected with deterioration of the premises as a direct result of misuse by the tenant.

Ground Five is that the landlord has arranged to sell or let the property because the tenant gave notice that he was giving up the tenancy.

Ground Six arises when the tenant has sub-let the premises, ie, has created another tenancy and is no longer the only tenant. Usually, the landlord will prohibit any sub-letting of a flat.

Ground Seven no longer exists.

Ground Eight is that the tenant was an employee of the landlord and the landlord requires the property for a new employee.

Ground Nine is where the landlord needs the property for himself or certain members of his family to live in.

Ground Ten is that a tenant has charged a subtenant more than the Rent Act permits.

One other important discretionary ground does not appear in the list of grounds in the 1977 Rent Act. It relates to the provision of suitable alternative accommodation. If the landlord requires possession of the property for reasons such as carrying out building works then it must be demonstrated that suitable alternative accommodation can be provided by the landlord for the tenant.

The mandatory grounds for possession of a property occupied by a protected tenant

These are grounds on which the court must give possession of a property to the landlord. The judge has no choice in the matter. If such an order is granted then it cannot be postponed for more than fourteen days, except where it would cause exceptional hardship when the maximum is six weeks. There are two basic rules for using the mandatory grounds:

1. The landlord must give a written notice saying that he/she may in future apply for possession under the appropriate ground. He/she must give it to the tenant normally when or before the tenancy begins (before the tenancy was granted, in the case of shorthold) and;

2. When he/she needs possession, the conditions of the appropriate ground must be met.

The mandatory grounds are as follows:

Ground Eleven. This ground is available only when the landlord has served notice at the beginning of the tenancy stating when he or she wants back the premises, ie, a date is specified.

Ground Twelve is valid only when a landlord has served notice that the property may be required for personal use as a retirement home.

Ground Thirteen applies only where the letting is for a fixed term of not more than eight months and it can be proved that the property was used as a holiday letting for twelve months before the letting began.

Ground Fourteen is that the accommodation was let for a fixed term of a year or less, having been let to students by a specified educational institution or body at some time during the previous twelve months.

Ground Fifteen is that the accommodation was intended for a clergyman and has been let temporarily to an ordinary client.

Ground Sixteen is that the accommodation was occupied by a farmworker and has been let temporarily to an ordinary tenant.

PRIVATE SECTOR AGREEMENTS SIGNED BEFORE JANUARY 1989 BUT WHICH DO NOT HAVE RENT ACT PROTECTION:

Not all people who entered into agreements before 15th January 1989 will be protected tenants under the 1977 Rent Act.

The licence

Private landlords have proved unwilling to accept protected tenants as it means that tenants will have the right to a low rent and will be difficult to get out. As a result, landlords have devised a number of loopholes which enable them to avoid granting a protected tenancy. One such arrangement is the licence agreement.

A licence is a personal arrangement between the landlord (licensor) and the licensee. The main difference between a licensee and a tenant is that the licensee, right from the beginning, has far less security than a tenant.

A licence to occupy a house, or part of a house, is the same, in principle, as a licence to drive a car or to run a public house. It gives permission to stay which is temporary and can be withdrawn.

Landlords find licences attractive because the protection which is given to tenants by the 1977 Rent Act and the 1988 Housing Act is not given to the licensee.

This means that the landlord can evict the licensee, without giving twenty eight days notice and without getting a court order. Or at least this seemed to be the case. Hardly surprising, then, that licences were so popular with landlords.

Courts have, until recently, looked upon licences quite favourably as long as both parties are aware of the meaning of the agreement.

In many cases, it goes without saying, the licensee did not understand the agreement. They did not understand that the agreement was temporary and meant that they could be evicted quite easily.

However, a number of court cases in the last few years have found that an agreement seeming to be a licence in fact amounted to a tenancy and therefore had protection.

In other words, the courts are taking a tougher view of landlords avoidance of protection for their tenants.

In court cases the landlord will be asked to prove that the agreement in question is in fact a licence. The main difference between a licence and a tenancy is quite simply that of exclusive possession. If the tenant has exclusive possession of even a room then an agreement can be held to be a tenancy and not a licence.

Other agreements signed before 1989 which are not protected

There are other types of agreement which will not be classed as a protected tenancy.

Tenancies granted before 14th August 1974, and which are furnished with a resident landlord

If a tenancy was entered into before the above date and the property was furnished to a reasonable standard it is not considered to be protected. This is another complex area and will not be pursued further here.

Restricted contracts under the 1977 Rent Act

A tenancy entered into before 15th January 1989 will not be

protected if, when the tenancy was first entered into, the landlord was still living in the same building as the property which has been let to the tenant. This is known as a restricted contract. The exception is the situation where the block is purpose-built and the landlord has a separate flat.

However, if one landlord sells his interest to another person who intends to live in the building, the tenancy will remain unprotected for twenty eight days. In that twenty eight days the person taking over the property can either take up residence or serve written notice that he intends to do so within the next six months.

As long as he/she takes up residence within six months the notice serves to prevent the tenancy becoming protected.

If a tenancy is not protected because it falls within the above category then it is known as a restricted contract. However, one important point is that a restricted contract will cease to be such after the passing of the 1988 Rent Act when there is a change in the amount of rent payable under the contract other than a change determined by the rent tribunal.

From then on, the restricted contract becomes an assured tenancy. More about assured tenancies later.

Flats and houses under certain rateable values

If the property has a rateable value of over £750 (£1,500 in Greater London) that property cannot be the subject of a protected tenancy. In practice, few properties are above this figure.

Even after the change from rateable values to community charge and the council tax in 1993, the rateable value of a property will still apply in this case.

Tenancies at low rents

A tenancy which was entered into before 1st April 1990 is not a protected tenancy if the rent paid is less than two-thirds of the rateable value of the property on the appropriate day. The appropriate day is 23rd March 1973 unless the property was valued at a later date. If no rent is paid then the tenancy will not be protected.

Flats and houses let with other land

If a property is let with other land to which it is only an adjunct (an addition) then it will not be a protected tenancy. However, importantly, unless the other land consists of more than two acres of agricultural land, it will be taken as part of the dwelling house and will not prevent the tenancy being protected.

Payments for board and attendance

If a part of the rent for which a house is let is payable in respect of board or attendance there will not be a protected tenancy.

Board, which is the provision of meals, must be more than minimal if the tenancy is not to be protected. Provision of a continental breakfast would be enough, whilst the provision of hot drinks would not.

Attendance includes personal services such as making beds. This provision is one that is often used by landlords to avoid the Rent Act. Such a tenancy, though, may form a restricted contract (see above).

Lettings to students

A tenancy granted by a specified educational institution to students studying will not be protected (the institution will usually be a university or college of further education).

Holiday lettings

A tenancy is not a protected tenancy if its purpose is to give the tenant the right to occupy the dwelling for a holiday.

Agricultural holdings

A tenancy is not protected if the dwelling is part of an agricultural holding and is occupied by the person responsible for the control of the farming of the holding. Tenancies of this sort are subject to the control of the Agricultural Holdings Act 1986 and other areas of the law.

Licensed premises

Where a tenancy of a dwelling house consists of or comprises premises licensed for the sales of alcohol, there will not be a protected tenancy.

Resident landlords

The tenancy will not be protected if, at the commencement of the tenancy, the landlord was resident in the same building as the property which has been let. This does not apply if the landlord merely has another flat in a purpose-built block; he must be in the same building or residence.

Where the landlord is a local authority, the Crown, a housing association or a co-operative

The tenancy will not be protected where the landlord is one of the above. Tenants of local authorities, housing associations, the Crown or a Co-operative have a different sort of protection, which this guide does not go into.

Company lets

Only an individual person is capable of living in a flat or house. If a property is let to a company there can be no statutory (legal) tenancy. When a property is let to a company, the tenancy would be between that company and a landlord. There are certain circumstances, however, where a company let can be a protected tenancy and the fair rent legislation applies.

6

Secure Tenancies

The 1980 Housing Act introduced the right to buy for public sector tenancies and also introduced a measure of protection hitherto absent. The 1985 Housing Act consolidated the 1980 Housing Act. Over the years since its inception, the 1985 Housing Act has been subject to a number of amendments, notably the 1988 Housing Act, which will be discussed later, and which shifted Housing Associations from the public sector to the private sector, but not local authorities.

Secure tenancies
The Housing Act 1985 s 79 (1) defines a secure tenancy as:

1) A tenancy under which a dwelling house is let as a separate dwelling is a secure tenancy at any time when the condition described in s 80 and 81 as the landlord condition and the tenant condition is satisfied.

There must be a tenancy of a dwelling house which is let as a separate dwelling. Unlike private sector legislation, the 1985 Housing Act does not exclude licences from statutory protection.

As far as security is concerned, a secure tenancy, as defined by the 1985 Act, will lose security if one of the conditions creating a secure tenancy is not present. We will be considering the conditions below. One of the main conditions, as we shall see, is that of maintaining the home as an only or principle home. Failure to do this, i.e. by residing elsewhere will render the tenancy non-secure.

However, if at a later date, the condition becomes satisfied, i.e. the tenant moves back in then security is retained (Hussey v Camden Council 1995 27 HLR.5 CA). Where possession proceedings are brought, in deciding whether security of tenure has been lost the courts will look at the situation that existed at the expiry of the notice to quit.

The landlord condition

The main factor that defines a secure tenancy is the status of the landlord. A landlord must be one of the prescribed bodies set out in the 1985 Housing Act s 80(1). The main landlord body issuing secure tenancies is a local authority. There are other bodies which can issue secure tenancies, such as a New Town Corporation, a Housing Action Trust, an Urban Development Corporation, the Development Board for Rural Wales and, in certain cases, some housing Co-operatives.

Before January 15th 1988, Housing Associations could grant secure tenancies. After this date, they cannot and secure tenancies will only exist in Housing Associations where they have been granted pre-1988, where immediately before the granting of a new tenancy the tenant was a secure tenant of the same landlord , where a mutual exchange occurs or where a tenant is transferred as part of a large scale voluntary stock transfer from local authority to housing association.

In addition, if a tenant has been granted suitable alternative accommodation by an order of the court, and the court deems the assured tenancy to be unsuitable a secure tenancy can be granted.

In the main, the number of secure tenancies in the housing association, or Registered Social Landlord sector have dwindled and are now in a minority.

The tenant condition

The Housing Act 1985 s 81 defines tenant condition as:

a) the tenant is an individual and occupies the dwelling house as his or her only or principal home; or

b) where the tenancy is a joint tenancy and each of the joint tenants is an individual and at least one of them occupies the dwelling as his or her only or principal home.

Shared accommodation

The definition in relation to the 1985 Act is stricter than the Rent Act 1977 and the Housing Act 1988. A tenant who shares a kitchen will not be a secure tenant for the purposes of the 1985 Act. The sharing of a bathroom however, will not take the tenant outside of the Act, because a bathroom is not seen as an essential living room.

Secure licences

The Housing Act 1985 s 79(3) provides that a licensee may be a secure tenant except for licences granted to those who occupy temporary accommodation. Although section 79(3) appears to give significant protection to licensees this protection was restricted by a decision of the House of Lords in Westminster City Council v Clarke (1992) 2 AC 288. In this case it was held that a licensee could be a secure tenant only if he or she had exclusive possession of a separate dwelling house. Mr Clarke, who occupied a room in a hostel was not held to be a secure tenant. Where licensees have a secure tenancy they cannot exercise the right to buy their properties, as afforded to other secure tenants. Section 79(3) of the Act states that it is only the provisions of that part of the act that apply to licensees and not the rest of the Act, including part 5 which contain the right to buy provisions.

Introductory tenancies

An introductory tenancy is one which would have been a secure tenancy but for the housing authority choosing to adopt the introductory tenancy regime. Introductory tenancies are used by local authorities where they have decided to use this device as a sort of probation, before offering a secure tenancy. There is a trial period of one year. This device, it is hoped, will go some way to ensuring good behaviour, particularly of the worst tenants, the so called 'problem families'.

Statutory exclusions from the Housing Act 1985

Schedule 1 of the Housing Act 1985 lists the types of tenancies that cannot be secure:

- Long leases-a fixed term tenancy granted for a term-certain exceeding 21 years cannot be a secure tenancy
- Introductory tenancies-are excluded from being secure tenancies by virtue of sch 1 para 1A (inserted by the Housing Act 1996).
- Premises occupied in connection with employment-under schedule 1, para 2 of the 1985 Act, if a tenant is either an employee of the landlord or an employee of one of the public bodies listed in para 2, and the premises is occupied in connection with that employment then the tenant cannot be a secure tenant.

  Even if the tenancy agreement does not specify that the tenancy is in connection with employment the court will infer that this is the case if the facts of the matter show it. If a tenant has secure status but his employment changes and the premises are seen as essential to his job then secure status will be lost. In Elvidge v Coventry Council (1993) 3 WLR 976, an employee was originally a secure tenant. He was promoted and his change in duties made it necessary the particular premises to carry out his job. The court held that he was no longer a secure tenant.

  If an employee retires, this does not mean that the occupier becomes a secure tenant. Employees are excluded from protection to enable the landlord to keep control of the premises for the job.

Land acquired for development

A tenancy cannot be a secure tenancy if the dwelling house is on land which has been acquired for development and the dwelling house is used by the landlord, pending development, as temporary accommodation. This exception will apply even if the land was acquired for development by the landlords predecessor in title (Hyde Housing Association v Harrison (1991) 1 EGLR S1.

However, if the development is no longer to be carried out, or in prospect, the reverse will apply (Lilleshall Housing Co-operative v Brennan (1992) 24 HLR 195).

When a person moves into an area to take up employment and accepts accommodation from a public landlord the landlord can deny secure status by virtue of sch 1 para 5 of the 1985 Housing Act. To achieve this the landlord must serve notice in writing that this exception applies. The exclusion will apply where, immediately before the grant of the tenancy the person was not resident in the area, an offer of employment was gained before the grant of the tenancy and the tenancy was granted to him/her for the purposes of meeting temporary accommodation.

If the landlord is a local housing authority the tenancy will not become secure until the housing authority has notified the tenant that it is secure. If the landlord is not a local housing authority, the tenancy will become secure after one year of grant, unless notified earlier.

Short-term arrangements

Sch 1 para 6 of the 1985 Act deals with short-term arrangements. Local authorities make arrangements with private landlords to help with finding homeless people or others, accommodation. Tenants of property sub-let from private landlords cannot therefore become secure tenants.

Other exclusions from the secure tenancy regime include:

- Temporary accommodation during works
- agricultural holdings
- licensed premises
- student lettings
- Business tenancies
- Almshouses

The terms of a secure tenancy

Although the terms of a secure tenancy are, to some extent, contractual, there are a number of terms included by statute. The Housing Act 1985 s 104 gives a public sector landlord an obligation to publish information about its secure tenancy. This will be an express term of the tenancy explaining matters such as the right to buy, right to repair, other repairing obligations etc. Section 105 of the Act places a further obligation on the landlord to consult tenants over matters of housing management.

Assigning a secure tenancy

There are certain rights to assign a secure tenancy:

- mutual exchange
- matrimonial or children related reasons where a court will assign
- assignment through succession

Exchange

Section 92 of the 1985 Housing Act implies a term into every secure tenancy that the tenant, subject to fulfilling certain criteria and with landlords consent can assign a tenancy by way of exchanging the tenancy with another tenant of a local authority or housing association. The criteria relate, for example, to the size of the property, i.e. whether under or over occupation will occur and also the tenants rent account and the condition of the property.

A landlord cannot unreasonably withhold consent if the parties to the exchange fulfil the criteria.

Matrimonial proceedings

The general prohibition on assignment does not apply to property adjustment orders made under s23 and 24 of the Matrimonial Causes Act 19 under 17(1) of the Matrimonial and Family Proceedings Act 1984. Where parties divorce the courts can make an order for the transfer of tenancy from one party to another.

Assignment to a potential successor

A secure tenant may assign a tenancy during his or her lifetime provide that the person to whom he or she assigns would be qualified to succeed to the tenancy on death (Housing Act 1985 s 91 (3) C.

Sub-letting of a secure tenancy

Under the HA 1985 s93, it is a term of every secure tenancy that:

a) the tenant may allow any persons to reside as lodgers, but;
b) will not, without the written consent of the landlord part with possession of part of the dwelling.

If the tenant parts with possession of the whole of the dwelling house then security of tenure is lost and cannot be regained and a notice to quit may be served ending the tenancy. A court order must be obtained before formal ending.

If a secure tenant applies to sub-let part of the dwelling then a landlord cannot unreasonably withhold permission.

Repairs and alterations under a secure tenancy

Under the 1985 HA s 96 the Secretary of State is entitled to introduce regulations to assist tenants whose landlords are local housing authorities to have 'qualifying repairs' carried out. A qualifying repair is one which the landlord is covenanted to carry out. The regulations (Secure Tenants of local housing authorities (Right to Repair) Regulations 1994 entitle the secure tenant to apply to the landlord to have a repair carried out. The landlord should then issue a repair notice specifying the nature of the repair, the identity of the contractor and the date by which the work should be carried cut. If the repair is not carried out by this date the tenant will be entitled to compensation.

Alterations

By s 97(1) of the 1985 Act, it is an implied term of every tenancy that the tenant shall not make alterations without the permission of the landlord. Consent cannot be held unreasonably. If it is withheld unreasonably then it will be treated as consent given. If the landlord neither grants nor gives consent within a reasonable time then consent is treated as being withheld.

A tenant who has improved property may be entitled to compensation if the improvements have added to the value of the property or the rent the landlord can charge. If the improvements were made before 1st February 1994. compensation will be governed by section 100 of the housing Act 1985. These provisions were amended by s122 of the Leasehold Reform Housing and Urban Development Act 1993, so compensation for improvements begun on 1st February 1994 will be governed by s 99A and 99B which were inserted into the HA 1985 by the 1993 Act.

Variation of a secure tenancy

Secure tenancy terms can be varied in three ways:

a) by agreement with the landlord and tenant
b) in accordance with the provisions of the tenancy agreement
c) in accordance with s 103 of the 1985 Act

Terms which have been implied by statute cannot be varied. Section 103 only applies to a secure periodic tenancy. It sets out the procedure to be followed by a landlord who wishes to vary a secure tenancy. This is achieved by notices governed by timescales.

Rent

The Housing Act 1985 contains no system of rent control, in contrast to the 1977 Rent Act. Local Authorities are entitled by section 24(1) of the 1985 Act to 'make such reasonable charges as they may determine for the tenancy or occupation'.

Security of tenure under the 1985 Act

The Housing Act 1985 restricts only the landlord's rights to end a secure tenancy. A tenant can still terminate a tenancy by use of a notice to quit. The tenancy will contain the process within which the tenant should give notice.

The landlord has to follow a strict process in order to determine a secure tenancy. If the tenancy is fixed term, the landlord will wait until the term has expired before taking possession. If the tenant does not vacate then a court order must be obtained, on one of the grounds for possession listed further on.

Periodic tenancies

Most secure tenancies are periodic tenancies. This cannot be brought to an end by service of a notice to quit. The landlord has to follow a set of procedures laid out in the 1985 Act s 83 and 83A.

Proceedings for possession can only be started if a notice of seeking possession, in accordance with s 83, has been served on the tenant. The main principle when serving notice is that the tenant has to receive the notice. This is known as 'proof of service'. The court may consider dispensing with a notice of seeking possession if it is just and equitable to do so. The notice of seeking possession must state the date after which court proceeding will begin, an application for possession applied for. Generally speaking, this is after 28 days but it is custom and practice to apply after the rent date (Monday) after the 28th day has expired. The notice remains in force for 12 months days after expiry. Proceedings cannot be brought under a notice after this time and a new notice must be served.

S83(2) provides that a notice seeking possession must:

a) be in a form prescribed by regulations made by the Secretary of State
b) specify the ground on which the court will be asked to make an order for possession of the dwelling house
c) give particulars of the ground

The information must be sufficient and clear enough for the tenant to understand and to remedy the breach of agreement.

The court cannot make an order for possession on a ground for possession unless it is stated in the notice, but the landlord may be ale to alter or add grounds with leave of the court.

If the landlord is attempting to recover possession under ground 2, for nuisance or other anti-social behaviour then a slightly different notice is required. This notice must state that proceedings for possession may be begun immediately and also specify the date sought by the landlord as the date by which the tenant must give up possession. The reason for the difference is that if a landlord is taking action for anti-social behaviour then the landlord may have to act quickly depending on the severity of the behaviour. See grounds for possession.

Succeeding to a secure tenancy

The Housing Act 1985 s 87 provides that a person is qualified to succeed to a secure tenancy if he or she occupies the dwelling as an only or principal home at the time of the tenants death and is either the tenants spouse or is a member of the tenants family and has resided at the property for a period of 12 months prior to death.

A tenants spouse will be entitled to succeed provide that he or she was occupying the marital home as principal home when the tenant died. A spouse means a married partner although a fairly recent decision in Ghaidan v Godan Mendoza (2003) 2 WLR 478 makes it seem likely that same sex couples living together must be treated equally to avoid discrimination under Article 14 of the European Convention for the Protection of Human Rights. The recent Civil Partnerships Act 2004 will also have a bearing on this.

A member of the tenant's family must fulfil the residence requirement of 12 months, i.e. living in the home for 12 months prior to death before succession is granted. Section 113 defines a member of the family as a spouse, a person who lives with the tenant as man and wife, parent, grandparent, child, grandchild, brother, sister, uncle, aunt, nephew and niece. It also provides that half blood relationships are to be regarded as whole blood, i.e. stepchildren and illegitimate children treated as legitimate. A de-facto spouse will be counted as a member of the family and has to fulfil the 12-month residence requirement.

The residence requirement for family members does not demand that the person living with the tenant lived in the property to which that person is seeking to succeed. For example, in Waltham Forest

69

Council v Thomas (1992) 2 AC 198, two brothers lived together for more than two and a half years and then moved to a new house. It was found that one brother was entitled to succeed to the secure tenancy when the other brother died 10 days after the move.

The Housing Act 1985 permits only one succession. If the deceased tenant was already a successor, no one will be able to succeed to the tenancy. A person who has become a sole tenant of a joint tenancy will be treated as a successor. Where a joint tenant becomes a sole tenant following death the remaining tenant will be deemed to be a successor.

If a tenant who is a successor is granted a new tenancy of the same dwelling house within six months of the end of the previous tenancy, that person will not be regarded as a successor.

If more than one person is entitled to succeed to a periodic secure tenancy, it is the spouse who will take precedence. If the deceased person had no spouse and has two or more family members entitled to succeed the family must decide amongst them. If no agreement can be reached the landlord will decide.

Where there is no person qualified to succeed, the tenancy will be disposed of either in the will of the tenant or to the intestacy rules. If this is the case the tenancy will cease to be a secure tenancy unless the vesting or disposal of the tenancy is in pursuance of an order made under s23 or 24 of the Matrimonial Causes Act 1974. Once a tenancy ceases to be secure security cannot be regained.

If the tenancy is for a fixed term it will be disposed of under a will or intestacy. The same rules as above apply.

Other provisions for secure tenants

Part V of the housing Act 1985 extends the right to buy to secure tenants. This enables tenants to buy their properties at a discount from local authority landlords.

Part V of the 1985 HA confers upon the secure tenant the right to buy either the freehold or to be granted a long lease of the dwelling house in which he or she is resident. A lease will normally be for 125 years with a low ground rent, typically £10.

The right to buy can belong to only a secure tenant or to a person closely connected to a secure tenant, for example, a family member. If the secure tenancy is a joint tenancy, the right to buy belongs jointly to all of the tenants or to one of them as may be agreed. Where there is only one secure tenant, that tenant may choose to share the right to buy with not more than three members of his or her family regardless of the fact that the family members are not joint tenants. To be eligible to share the right to buy a family member must be a tenant's spouse, a family member who has been residing with the tenant for 12 months previously or a family member to whom the landlord has consented to the right to buy.

Tenants must satisfy a qualifying period as a resident which is currently five years (after July 2005. The qualifying period does not have to be with one landlord but can be with any number of social landlords.

Excluded properties from the right to buy

The Housing Act 1985 s 120 provides that the right to buy will not arise in the cases specified in sch 5 to the Act. The most important exceptions are as follows:

a) the landlord is a charitable housing trust or association

b) the landlord is a co-operative housing association

c) the landlord is a housing association which has never received a grant of public funds

d) the landlord does not own the freehold or an interest sufficient to grant a lease 21 years in the case of a house or 50 years for a flat

e) where the dwelling house forms part of a building which is held mainly for purposes other than housing and was let to the tenant in consequence of the tenants employment by the landlord.

f) where the dwelling house was designed or altered to make it suitable for occupation by physically disabled persons

g) where the dwelling house is one of a group of dwelling houses which it is the practice of the landlord to let for occupation by persons who suffer a mental disorder and social services and special facilities are provided

h) Wher the dwelling house is one of a group of dwelling houses particularly suitable for elderly persons and special facilities are provided.

Section 21 provides also that the right to buy cannot be exercised where a court order is in effect and the tenant is obliged to give up possession of the dwelling house or the person, or one of the persons who have the right to buy is an undischarged bankrupt or has a bankruptcy provision pending against them or has made a composition or an arrangement with his or her creditors the terms of which remain unfulfilled.

The preserved right to buy

Tenants will retain their right to buy in the event of a large scale voluntary transfer of housing stock from a local authority to a housing association, or other body set up to take the transfer. Section 171 (b) of the 1985 guarantees the right to buy, known a the preserved right to buy with certain modifications as long as the tenant continues to occupy the property a their only or principal home.

Procedure for the right to buy

A strict notice-driven procedure is in place for the exercise of the right to buy. The tenant will apply initially using an RTB1 form. The initial application can be withdrawn at any time up to completion.

If after notice has been given and there is a change of tenant the new tenant will be treated as if he or she had given the notice. This is relevant to circumstances such as succession or other legitimate assignment. The new tenant will also be eligible for the discount claimed in the notice by the former tenant. Likewise, if there is a new landlord the new landlord is placed in the position that the old one was in.

Once a notice has been served the landlord will have four weeks to reply or eight in the case of having to apply to different landlords for a reference to fulfil the residency criteria. Within this period the landlord will either admit or deny the right to buy.

Using form RTB2.

Following the issue of the RTB2 the landlord will, if the RTB has been admitted, serve a s125 notice stating details of purchase price, original valuation and discount and also the costs of major repairs and decorations over the next five years. This is an important notice, tying the landlord in to a fixed service charge in respect of major repairs The landlord has eight weeks to produce this notice of freehold and twelve weeks if leasehold.

The tenant can dispute the valuation carried out by valuers instructed by the landlord and can appeal to the district valuer whose findings are final.

The tenant must serve a further notice on the landlord within twelve weeks of receiving the s125 notice. The notice must state whether or not the tenant intends to pursue the RTB or whether to withdraw the claim. If a notice is received but the tenant still does not pursue the claim the landlord will serve a prior notice to complete which gives the tenant 56 days to complete. If this period elapses then the landlord will serve a final notice which gives the tenant 56 days to complete. After this final period the landlord will withdraws the offer.

The price payable for the property in question will be the open market valuation less discount. The amount of discount has changed. In London for example, where the discounts used to be in line with the rest of the country, it is now a flat £16,000. In addition, if a tenant sells their property within five years then a proportion f the discount, gradually reducing, is repayable.

The Right to Acquire for tenants of registered social landlords

In order to overcome the problem of those people who do not qualify for the right to buy, i.e. the vast majority of housing Association Tenants on assured tenancies, the government introduced the right to acquire for tenants of registered social landlords. This was introduced by the Housing Act 1996. Tenants who have occupied housing association property for two years or more, on a secure or assured tenancy, will have the right to buy if their property was built with public funds or substantially refurbished with public funds after April 1997. There are some exceptions to the right to acquire, such as properties in rural areas and properties which have been specially adapted.

The 1985 Act Grounds for Possession of a secure tenancy

As with all tenancies, if there is a breach of agreement, the landlord will need to take action to end that agreement. In the case of secure tenancies there are 17 grounds for possession which the landlord can rely on.

1. Grounds for possession

Grounds 1 - 8: Grounds on which the Court may order possession if it considers it reasonable

Ground 1: Rent arrears or other breach of tenancy

Rent lawfully due from the tenant has not been paid or an obligation of the tenancy has been broken or not performed.

Ground 2: Nuisance

The tenant or a person residing in or visiting the dwelling-house-

- has been guilty of conduct causing or likely to cause a nuisance or annoyance to a person residing, visiting or otherwise engaging in a lawful activity in the locality, or
- has been convicted of-using the dwelling-house or allowing it to be used for immoral or illegal purposes, or an arrestable offence committed in, or in the locality of, the dwelling house.

Ground 2A: Domestic Violence

The dwelling-house was occupied (whether alone or with other) by a married couple or a couple living together as husband and wife and –

- one or both of the partners is a tenant of the dwelling-house, one partner has left because of violence or threats of violence by the other towards that partner, or a member of the family of that partner who was residing with that partner immediately before the partner left, and the court is satisfied that the partner who has left is unlikely to return.

Ground 3: Waste and neglect

The condition of the dwelling-house or of any of the common parts has deteriorated owing to acts of waste by, or neglect or default of, the tenant or a person residing in the dwelling-house and, in the case of an act of waste by, or neglect or default of, a person lodging with the tenant or a sub-tenant of his the tenant has not taken such steps as he ought reasonably to have taken for the removal of the lodger or sub-tenant.

Ground 4: Damage to furniture

The condition of furniture provided by the landlord for use under the tenancy, or for use in the common parts, has deteriorated owing to ill-treatment by the tenant or a person residing in the dwelling-house and, in the case of ill-treatment by a person lodging with the tenant or a sub-tenant of his, the tenant has not taken such steps as he ought reasonably to have taken for the removal of the lodger or sub-tenant.

Ground 5: Misrepresentation

The tenant is the person, or one of the persons. to whom the tenancy was granted and the landlord was induced to grant the tenancy by a false statement made knowingly or recklessly by-

- the tenant, or
- a person acting at the tenant's instigation

Ground 6: Premium on assignment

The tenancy was assigned to the tenant, or a predecessor in title of his who is a member of his family and is residing in the dwelling-house, by an assignment made by virtue of section 92 (assignments by way of exchange) and a premium was paid either in connection with that assignment or the assignment which the tenant or predecessor himself made by virtue of that section.

In this paragraph 'premium' means any fine or other like sum and any pecuniary consideration in addition to rent.

Ground 7: Misconduct in tied accommodation

The dwelling-house forms part of, or is within the curtilage of, a building which, or so much of it as is held by the landlord, is held mainly for purposes other than housing purposes and consists mainly of accommodation other than housing accommodation, and-

- the dwelling-house was let to the tenant or a predecessor in title of his in consequence of the tenant or predecessor being in the employment of the landlord, or of a local authority, a new town corporation , a housing action trust an urban development corporation the Development Board for Rural Wales, or the governors of an aided school, and

- the tenant or a person residing in the dwelling-house has been guilty of conduct such that, having regard to the purpose for which the building is used, it would not be right for him to continue in occupation of the dwelling house.

Ground 8: Temporary housing during repairs

The dwelling-house was made available for occupation by the tenant (or a predecessor in title of his) while works were carried out on the dwelling-house which he previously occupied as his only or principal home and –

- the tenant (or predecessor) was a secure tenant of the other dwelling-house at the time when he ceased to occupy it as his home,

- the tenant (or predecessor) accepted the tenancy of the dwelling-house of which possession is sought on the understanding that he would give up occupation when, on completion of the works, the other dwelling-house was again available for occupation by him under a secure tenancy, and

- the works have been completed and the other dwelling-house is so available.

Grounds 9 - 11: Grounds on which the Court may order possession if suitable alternative accommodation is available

Ground 9: Overcrowding

The dwelling-house is overcrowded within the meaning of Part X, in such circumstances as to render the occupier guilty of an offence.

Ground 10: Demolition, reconstruction, or major works

The landlord intends , within a reasonable time of obtaining possession of the dwelling-house-

- to demolish or reconstruct the building or part of the building comprising the dwelling-house, or

- to carry out work on that building or on land let together with, and thus treated as part of, the dwelling-house,

- and cannot reasonably do so without obtaining possession of the dwelling-house.

Ground 10A: Redevelopment scheme

The dwelling house is in an area which is the subject of a redevelopment scheme approved by the Secretary of State or the Housing Corporation in accordance with Part V of this Schedule and the landlord intends within a reasonable time of obtaining possession to dispose of the dwelling-house in accordance with this scheme.

or

Part of the dwelling-house is in such an area and the landlord intends within a reasonable time of obtaining possession to dispose of that part in accordance with the scheme and for that purpose reasonably requires possession of the dwelling-house.

Ground 11: Charitable landlord

The landlord is a charity and the tenant's continued occupation of the dwelling house would conflict with the objects of the charity.

Grounds 12 - 16: Grounds on which the Court may order possession if it considers it reasonable and suitable alternative accommodation is available

Ground 12: Tied accommodation

The dwelling-house forms part of, or is within the curtilage of, a building which, or so much of it as is held by the landlord, is held mainly for the purposes other than housing purposes and consists mainly of accommodation other than housing accommodation, or is situated in a cemetery, and-

- the dwelling-house was let to the tenant or a predecessor in title of his in consequence of the tenant or predecessor being in the employment of the landlord or of a local authority, a new town corporation a housing action trust, an urban development corporation the Development Board for Rural Wales, or the governors of an aided school, and that employment has ceased, and

- the landlord reasonably requires the dwelling-house for occupation as a residence for some person either engaged in the employment of the landlord, or of such a body, or with whom a contract for such employment has been entered into conditional on housing being provided.

Ground 13: Accommodation for disabled persons

The dwelling-house has features which are substantially different from those of ordinary dwelling-houses and which are designed to make it suitable for occupation by a physically disabled person who requires accommodation of a kind provided by the dwelling-house and- there is no longer such a person residing in the dwelling-house, and the landlord requires it for occupation (whether alone or with members of his family) by such a person.

78

Ground 14: Accommodation for special groups

The landlord is a housing association or housing trust which lets dwelling-houses only for occupation (whether alone or with others) by persons whose circumstances (other than merely financial circumstances) make it especially difficult for them to satisfy their need for housing, and-

- either there is no longer such a person residing in the dwelling-house or the tenant has received from a local housing authority an offer of accommodation in premises which are to be let as a separate dwelling-house under a secure tenancy, and

- the landlord requires the dwelling-house for occupation (whether alone or with members of his family) by such a person.

Ground 15: Accommodation for special needs

The dwelling-house is one of a group of dwelling-houses which it is the practice of the landlord to let for occupation by persons with special needs-

- a social service or special facility is provided in close proximity to the group of dwelling-houses in order to assist in persons with those special needs,

- there is no longer a person with those special needs residing in the dwelling-house, and

- the landlord requires the dwelling-house for occupation (whether alone or with members of his family) by a person who has those special needs.

Ground 16: Under-occupation by successor

The accommodation afforded by the dwelling-house is more extensive than is reasonably required by the tenant and- the tenancy vested in the tenant by virtue of section 89 (succession to periodic tenancy), the tenant being qualified to succeed by virtue of section 87(b) (members of family other than spouse), and

- notice of the proceedings for possession was served under section 83 (or, where no such notice was served, the proceedings for possession were begun) more than six months but less than twelve months after the date of the previous tenant's death.

- The matter to be taken into account by the court in determining whether it is reasonable to make an order on this ground include-the age of the tenant, the period during which the tenant has occupied the dwelling-house as his only or principal home, and any financial or other support given by the tenant to the previous tenant.

7

The 1988 Housing Act-Assured Tenancies

The assured tenant

As we have seen, with the exception of local authority tenancies and a few remaining Rent Act protected tenancies, all tenancies, (with the main exceptions detailed), signed after Jan 15th 1989, are known as assured tenancies. An assured shorthold tenancy, which is the most common form of tenancy used by private landlords nowadays, is one type of assured tenancy, and is for a fixed term of six months minimum and can be brought to an end with two months notice by serving a section 21 (of the Housing Act 1988) notice.

It is important to note that all tenancies signed after February 1997 are assured shorthold agreements unless otherwise stated in the agreement.

Assured tenancies are governed by the 1988 Housing Act, as amended by the 1996 Housing Act. It is to these Acts, or outlines of the Acts that the tenant must refer when intending to sign a tenancy for a residential property.

For a tenancy to be assured, three conditions must be fulfilled:
1. The premises must be a dwelling house. This basically means any premises which can be lived in. Business premises will normally fall outside this interpretation.
2. There must exist a particular relationship between landlord and tenant. In other words there must exist a tenancy agreement. For example, a licence to occupy, as in the case of students, or accommodation occupied as a result of work, cannot be seen as a tenancy. Following on from this, the accommodation must be let as a single unit. The tenant, who must be an individual, must normally be able to sleep, cook and eat in the accommodation.

Sharing of bathroom facilities will not prevent a tenancy being an assured tenancy but shared cooking or other facilities, such as a living room, will.

2. The third requirement for an assured tenancy is that the tenant must occupy the dwelling as his or her only or principal home. In situations involving joint tenants at least one of them must occupy.

Tenancies that are not assured

A tenancy agreement will not be assured if one of the following conditions applies:

-The tenancy or the contract was entered into before 15th January 1989;

-If no rent is payable or if only a low rent amounting to less than two thirds of the present ratable value of the property is payable;

-If the premises are let for business purposes or for mixed residential and business purposes;

-If part of the dwelling house is licensed for the sale of liquor for consumption on the premises. This does not include the publican who lets out a flat;

-If the dwelling house is let with more than two acres of agricultural land;

-If the dwelling house is part of an agricultural holding and is occupied in relation to carrying out work on the holding;

-If the premises are let by a specified institution to students, i.e., halls of residence;

-If the premises are let for the purpose of a holiday;

-Where there is a resident landlord, e.g., in the case where the landlord has let one of his rooms but continues to live in the house;

-If the landlord is the Crown or a government department. Certain lettings by the Crown are capable of being assured, such as some lettings by the Crown Estate Commissioners;

-If the landlord is a local authority, a fully mutual housing association (this is where you have to be a shareholder to be a tenant) a newly created Housing Action Trust or any similar body listed in the 1988 Housing Act.

-If the letting is transitional such as a tenancy continuing in its original form until phased out, such as:

-A protected tenancy under the 1977 Rent Act;

-Secure tenancy granted before 1st January 1989, e.g., from a local authority or housing association. These tenancies are governed by the 1985 Housing Act.

The Assured Shorthold tenancy

The assured shorthold tenancy as we have seen, is the most common form of tenancy used in the private sector. The main principle of the assured shorthold tenancy is that it is issued for a period of six months minimum and can be brought to an end by the landlord serving two-months notice on the tenant. At the end of the six-month period the tenant, if given two months prior notice, must leave.

Any property let on an assured tenancy can be let on an assured shorthold, providing the following three conditions are met:

- The tenancy must be for a fixed term of not less than six months.
- The agreement cannot contain powers which enable the landlord to end the tenancy before six months. This does not include the right of the landlord to enforce the grounds for possession, which will be approximately the same as those for the assured tenancy (see below).
- A notice requiring possession at the end of the term is usually served two months before that date.
- A notice must be served before any rent increase giving one months clear notice and providing details of the rent increase.

If the landlord wishes to get possession of his/her property, in this case before the expiry of the contractual term, the landlord has to gain a court order. A notice of seeking possession must be served, giving fourteen days notice and following similar grounds of possession as an assured tenancy.

The landlord cannot simply tell a tenant to leave before the end of the agreed term.

If the tenancy runs on after the end of the fixed term then the landlord can regain possession by giving the required two months notice, as mentioned above.

At the end of the term for which the assured shorthold tenancy has been granted, the landlord has an automatic right to possession.

An assured shorthold tenancy will become periodic (will run from week to week) when the initial term of six months has elapsed and the landlord has not brought the tenancy to an end. A periodic tenancy is brought to an end with two months notice.

Assured shorthold tenants can be evicted only on certain grounds, some discretionary, some mandatory (see below).

In order for the landlord of an assured shorthold tenant to regain possession of the property, a notice of seeking possession (of property) must be served, giving fourteen days notice of expiry and stating the ground for possession.

Following the fourteen days a court order must be obtained. Although gaining a court order is not complicated, a solicitor will usually be used. Court costs can be awarded against the tenant.

Security of tenure: The ways in which a tenant can lose their home as an assured tenant

There are a number of circumstances called grounds (mandatory and discretionary) whereby a landlord can start a court action to evict a tenant.

The following are the *mandatory* grounds (where the judge must give the landlord possession) and *discretionary* grounds (where the judge does not have to give the landlord possession) on which a court can order possession if the home is subject to an assured tenancy.

The mandatory grounds for possession of a property let on an assured tenancy

There are eight mandatory grounds for possession, which, if proved, leave the court with no choice but to make an order for possession. It is very important that you understand these.

Ground One is used where the landlord has served a notice, no later than at the beginning of the tenancy, warning the tenant that this ground may be used against him/her.

This ground is used where the landlord wishes to recover the property as his or her principal (first and only) home or the spouse's (wife's or husbands) principal home.

The ground is not available to a person who bought the premises for gain (profit) whilst they were occupied.

Ground Two is available where the property is subject to a mortgage and if the landlord does not pay the mortgage, could lose the home.

Grounds Three and Four relate to holiday lettings.

Ground Five is a special one, applicable to ministers of religion.

Ground Six relates to the demolition or reconstruction of the property.

Ground Seven applies if a tenant dies and in his will leaves the tenancy to someone else: but the landlord must start proceedings against the new tenant within a year of the death if he wants to evict the new tenant.

Ground Eight concerns rent arrears. This ground applies if, both at the date of the serving of the notice seeking possession and at the date of the hearing of the action, the rent is at least 8 weeks in arrears or two months in arrears. This is the main ground used by landlords when rent is not being paid.

The discretionary grounds for possession of a property, which is let on an assured tenancy

As we have seen, the discretionary grounds for possession are those in relation to which the court has some powers over whether or not the landlord can evict. In other words, the final decision is left to the judge. Often the judge will prefer to grant a suspended order first, unless the circumstances are dramatic.

Ground Nine applies when suitable alternative accommodation is available or will be when the possession order takes effect. As we have seen, if the landlord wishes to obtain possession of his or her property in order to use it for other purposes then suitable alternative accommodation has to be provided.

Ground Ten deals with rent arrears as does *ground eleven*. These grounds are distinct from the mandatory grounds, as there does not have to be a fixed arrear in terms of time scale, e.g., 8 weeks. The judge, therefore, has some choice as to whether or not to evict. In practice, this ground will not be relevant to managers of assured shorthold tenancies.

Ground Twelve concerns any broken obligation of the tenancy. As we have seen with the protected tenancy, there are a number of conditions of the tenancy agreement, such as the requirement not to racially or sexually harass a neighbor. Ground Twelve will be used if these conditions are broken.

Ground Thirteen deals with the deterioration of the dwelling as a result of a tenant's neglect. This is connected with the structure of the property and is the same as for a protected tenancy. It puts the responsibility on the tenant to look after the premises.

Ground Fourteen concerns nuisance, annoyance and illegal or immoral use. This is where a tenant or anyone connected with the tenant has caused a nuisance to neighbors.

Ground 14A this ground deals with domestic violence.

Ground 15 concerns the condition of the furniture and tenants neglect. As Ground thirteen puts some responsibility on the tenant to look after the structure of the building so Ground Fifteen makes the tenant responsible for the furniture and fittings.

Ground 16 covers former employees. The premises were let to a former tenant by a landlord seeking possession and the tenant has ceased to be in that employment.

Ground 17 is where a person or that persons agents makes a false Or reckless statement and this has caused the landlord to grant the tenancy under false pretences.

The description of the grounds above is intended as a guide only. For a fuller description please refer to the 1988 Housing Act, section 7, Schedule two,) as amended by the 1996 Housing Act) which is available at reference libraries.

Fast track possession

In November 1993, following changes to the County Court Rules, a facility was introduced which enabled landlords of tenants with assured shorthold tenancies to apply for possession of their property without the usual time delay involved in waiting for a court date and attendance at court. This is known as "fast track possession" It cannot be used for rent arrears or other grounds. It is used to gain possession of a property when the fixed term of six months or more has come to an end and the tenant will not move.

Payment of rent

If the landlord wishes to raise rent, at least one month's minimum notice must be given. The rent cannot be raised more than once for the same tenant in one year. Tenants have the right to challenge a rent increase if they think it is unfair by referring the rent to a Rent Assessment Committee. The committee will prevent the landlord from raising the rent above the ordinary market rent for that type of property. We will be discussing rent and rent control further on in this book.

8

Joint Tenancies

Joint tenancies: the position of two or more people who have a tenancy agreement for one property

Although it is the normal state of affairs for a tenancy agreement to be granted to one person, this is not always the case.

A tenancy can also be granted to two or more people and is then known as a *joint tenancy*. The position of joint tenants is exactly the same as that of single tenants. In other words, there is still one tenancy even though it is shared.

Each tenant is responsible for paying the rent and observing the terms and conditions of the tenancy agreement. No one joint tenant can prevent another joint tenants access to the premises.

If one of the joint tenants dies then his or her interest will automatically pass to the remaining joint tenants. A joint tenant cannot dispose of his or her interest in a will.

If one joint tenant, however, serves a notice to quit (notice to leave the property) on another joint tenant(s) then the tenancy will come to an end and the landlord can apply to court for a possession order, if the remaining tenant does not leave.

The position of a wife or husband in relation to joint tenancies is rather more complex because the married person has more rights when it comes to the home than the single person.

Remember: the position of a tenant who has signed a joint tenancy agreement is exactly the same as that of the single tenant. If one person leaves, the other(s) have the responsibilities of the tenancy. If one person leaves without paying his share of the rent then the other tenants will have to pay instead.

9

The Law and Mobile Homes

If you own a mobile home, rent a pitch for it on a site and use it as your main residence, you will be protected by the Mobile Homes Act 1983. If you rent the home you will be covered by the law for tenants. The Act does not cover you if you only rent the home for holidays.

Protection from eviction
The Mobile Homes Act 1983 gives owners the right to keep their homes on the site they occupy indefinitely. There can only be a fixed time limit on the agreement if the site owner's planning permission, or right to use the land, is itself limited to a fixed period. If the time limit is later extended, then so is your right to stay there. The resident can bring the agreement to an end by giving at least four weeks notice in writing. The site owner can only bring the agreement to an end by applying to the county court or to an arbitrator. There are only three grounds on which the site owner can seek to end an agreement:

- You are not living in the mobile home as your main residence.
- The mobile home is having a detrimental effect on the site because of its age or condition or is likely to have this effect within the next five years. The site owner can only try to use this ground for ending the agreement once in any five-year period, starting from the date the agreement began.
- You have broken one of the terms of the agreement and the court or the arbitrator thinks it is reasonable to end the agreement. The site owner must first tell you that you have broken the agreement and give you a reasonable time to put things right.

If the site owner can prove to the court or the arbitrator that the agreement should be brought to an end for one of these reasons, the site owner can then get an eviction order from the courts. Arbitrators cannot make eviction orders. The site owner can normally go to court to end the agreement and for an eviction order at the same time.

If the site is privately owned, the court can suspend an eviction order for up to one year, but cannot suspend it if the site is owned by the local council. It is a criminal offence for the site owner to evict you without a court order, to harass or threaten you or to cut off services such as gas, electricity or water in order to get you to leave.

The site owner can only make you move to another part of the site if:

- Your agreement says that this can be done
- The new pitch is broadly comparable to the old one
- The site owner pays all the costs.

The right to a written agreement and a statement of rights
The site owner must give you a statement of your legal rights and the terms of your agreement. The agreement cannot change your rights under the Mobile Homes Act. You or the site owner can apply to change the terms of the agreement within six months of the issue of the original agreement. Either side can apply to the county court or an arbitrator, if they cannot agree the terms. You should always check the agreement for the terms of payment and fees and if not happy apply to change them.

Other rights of mobile home owners
You can sell your home and pass on the agreement with the site owner to a person of your choice. You can also give your home to a member of your family. In either case, the new owner must be approved by the site owner, but this approval cannot be unreasonably withheld. If this is the case then you can apply to the county court or an arbitrator for an order for the site owner to give approval. If you sell your home the site owner can claim a

commission of up to 20% of the price. If you die members of your family who were living with you will automatically inherit the agreement with the site owner and your legal rights.

10

Owner Occupiers and Service Charges

The Role of Service Charges

By far the commonest cause of dispute between leaseholders and freeholders is the provision of services and, especially, the levying of service charges. In extreme cases, leaseholders have been asked to contribute thousands of pounds towards the cost of major repairs, and have even suffered forfeiture of the lease if they are unable, or unwilling, to comply. Happily, such instances are rare; but even where the service charges are more moderate, they are often resented by leaseholders. The purpose of this Chapter is to explain the legitimate purpose of service charges and the legal obligations of both the leaseholder and the freeholder, and to offer some warnings about the circumstances where very high service charges are likely to be found.

The difference between long leases and tenancies (short-term and periodic) has been set out in previous chapters. One of its most important consequences is that services are paid for in a very different way. In a periodic or short-term tenancy, all the basic costs of providing and managing the housing are paid out of the rent. It is true that there will sometimes be a service charge as well, but it normally covers things such as the provision of heating or communal lighting - things that, however necessary they may be, are peripheral to the central function of providing housing. As a result, service charges in rented property are usually quite moderate and cause little argument.

Contrast the position in leasehold housing. In both types of housing, the landlord is under a legal obligation to the residents to keep the property in good condition and to carry out any work necessary for that purpose; but the landlord of rented property is expected to meet the costs from the rent, whereas the freeholder of leasehold stock has no rent to fall back on (apart from the normally negligible ground rent). How, then, are major costs to be met when they arise? The answer, of course, is from the service charge, which is, therefore, of central importance to the management of leasehold property.

From the freeholder's point of view, the logic of service charges is impeccable. It is perfectly reasonable for freeholders to point out:

- that leaseholders benefit from the work because it has maintained or improved their homes; and

- that the fact that the work has been done means that leaseholders will get a better price when they come to sell; and

- that people that own their homes freehold have to find the money to meet costs of this kind.

To sum up the freeholder's position: the costs have been incurred; the work is for the benefit of the leaseholders; so the leaseholders must pay.

Leaseholders can point out in reply that someone that owns his home freehold can make his own choice when and how to do the repair; he can put up with a slightly leaking roof if he cannot afford to repair it. But freeholders of leasehold property have no such discretion: they are obliged under the lease to do their repairs promptly and if they did not would be liable to legal action by any leaseholder. So it is difficult for leaseholders to object to the principle of charges or to ask the freeholder to refrain from carrying out work or to delay it. In short, the purchase of a lease means the acceptance of a commitment to pay the appropriate share of costs. But does this mean that leaseholders have no scope to challenge or query service charges? No; under sections 18 to 30 of the Landlord and Tenant Act 1985, amended by the 1996 Housing Act and the 2002 Commonhold and Leasehold Reform Act they have extensive legal protection against improper or unreasonable charging by freeholders, and this is discussed later in the Chapter.

Unreasonable Service Charges
a: General Principles

Sections 18 to 30 of the Landlord and Tenant Act 1985, as amended by subsequent legislation, grant substantial protection to leaseholders of residential property. This protection was introduced after complaints of exploitation by unscrupulous leaseholders, who were alleged to be carrying out unnecessary, or even fictitious, repairs at extravagant prices, whilst not providing the information that would have enabled leaseholders to query the bill. The general effect of the Act is to require freeholders to provide leaseholders with full information about service charges and to consult them before expensive works are carried out. It must be stressed, however, that although the Act protects leaseholders against sharp practice by freeholders, and will prevent the recovery of *unreasonable* costs, it will support freeholders, provided they have gone through the necessary formalities described below, in the recovery of their *reasonable* costs, even if those costs are high. To take the example used above of the removal of asbestos from a block of flats: the fact that the average cost per flat is as high as £50,000 does not, in itself, make the charge unreasonable - to make use of the Act, objecting leaseholders have to show, when they are notified that the work is to be carried out (not when the bills arrive), that it was not necessary or could have been carried out cheaper.

A few leases, namely those granted under the right to buy by local authorities or registered housing associations, have some additional protection under the Housing Act 1985 (see below), but sections 18 to 30 apply to all residential leases where the service charge depends on how much the freeholder spends. They set out the key rules that freeholders must observe in order to recover the cost, including overheads, of 'services, repairs or improvements, maintenance or insurance', as well as the freeholder's costs of management. Sections 18 to 30 only apply to service charges, not to other charges such as ground rent.

It should be noted that failure by leaseholders to pay the service charge does not relieve the freeholder of the obligation to provide the services. The freeholder's remedy is to sue the leaseholder for the outstanding charges, or even to seek forfeiture of the lease (see below). Section 19 of the Act provides the key protection to leaseholders by laying down that service charges are recoverable only if they are 'reasonably incurred' and if the services or works are of a reasonable standard. This means that the charge:

-   must relate to some form of service, repair, maintenance, improvement, or insurance that the freeholder is required to provide under the lease;
-   must be reasonable (that is, the landlord may not recover costs incurred unnecessarily or extravagantly);
-   may cover overheads and management costs only if these too are reasonable.

In addition, the charge must normally be passed on to the leaseholders within 18 months of being incurred, and in some cases the freeholder must consult leaseholders before spending the money. These points are covered below.

The Housing Act 1996 gave leaseholders new powers to refer service charges to the Leasehold Valuation Tribunal (LVT). This is covered below (*Challenging Service Charges*).

b: Consultation with Leaseholders
Section 20 as amended by the 2002 Commonhold and Leasehold Reform Act, provides extra protection where the cost of works is more than a certain limit. (£250 or more to the leaseholder). Costs above this level are irrecoverable unless the freeholder has taken steps to inform and consult tenants, although there are a exceptions in special cases (see below). If the leaseholders are not represented by a recognised tenants' association (for which see below) these steps are as follows:

Intention to carry out works: The landlord must write to all leaseholders stating the intention and reasons for carrying out work. There must be a notice period of 30 days.

Estimates At least two estimates must be obtained, of which at least one must be from someone wholly unconnected from the freeholder (obviously a building firm that the freeholder owns or works for is not 'wholly unconnected'; nor is the freeholder's managing agent. Arguably, even a building firm with which the freeholder has no formal connexion could be 'connected' with him if he gives it so much work that it depends on him and is thus subject to his influence)

Notification to leaseholders The freeholder must either display a copy of the estimates somewhere they are likely to be seen by everyone liable to pay the service charges or preferably send copies to everyone liable to pay the charge

Consultation The notification must describe the works to be carried out and must seek comments and observations, giving a deadline for replies and an address in the UK to which they may be sent. The deadline must be at least a month after the notice was sent or displayed.

Freeholder's response The freeholder must 'have regard' to representations received. This does not mean, of course, that the freeholder must do what the leaseholders say. It does mean, however, that the freeholder must consider any comments received, and good freeholders often demonstrate that they have done so by sending a reasoned reply (i.e. not a form letter or bare acknowledgment, but a letter that responds specifically to any points made), even though the Act does not require them to.

It was mentioned above that there are special cases in which these requirements can be set aside. If a service charge is challenged, it is defence for the freeholder to show that the works were so urgent that there was no time for proper consultation. It is also possible for freeholders to enter into long term agreements to carry out works or provide services over a period of years; if so, they must consult before the agreement is entered into but they need not consult separately before each particular element of expenditure under the agreement. Finally, the Leasehold Valuation Tribunal has a general power to set aside the usual consultation requirements if it seems fair to do so. Section 20 is important because it gives the leaseholders notification of any unusual items in the offing and gives them an opportunity to raise any concerns and objections. If the leaseholder has any reservations at all, it is vital that they be put before the freeholder at this stage. It is unlikely, in the event of legal action later, that courts or LVTs will support a leaseholder that raised no objection until the bill arrived.

It is surprisingly common for freeholders and their agents to fail to comply with the requirements of section 20. This comment applies not only where the freehold is owned by an individual or a relatively small organisation (where mistakes might be more understandable) but also where the freeholder is a large, well resourced body like a local authority (which should be well able to understand and carry out its legal duties).

As a result leaseholders are often paying service charges that are not due, so all leaseholders should, before paying a service charge containing unusual items, ensure that section 20, if it applies, has been scrupulously followed. If not, they can refuse to pay.

c: Other Protection for Leaseholders
Grant-aided works: If the freeholder has received a grant towards the cost of carrying out the works, the amount must be deducted from the service charge levied on leaseholders.

Late charging: Service charge bills may not normally include costs incurred more than eighteen months earlier. The freeholder may, however, notify leaseholders within the eighteen month period that they will have to pay a certain cost, and then bill them later. This may happen if, for instance, the freeholder is in dispute with a contractor about the level of a bill or the standard of work.

Pre-charging: Sometimes a lease will contain a provision allowing the freeholder to make a charge to cover future costs besides those already incurred. This practice, which is perfectly lawful in itself, may be in the interests of the leaseholders by spreading over a longer period the cost of major works. It is, however, subject to the same overall requirement of reasonableness.

Court costs: Section 20C provides protection against a specific abuse of the service charge system by freeholders. Previously, freeholders tended to regard their legal costs as part of the process of managing the housing and thus as recoverable from leaseholders. Such an attitude is not necessarily unreasonable: if, for instance, the freeholder is suing a builder for poor work, he is, in effect, acting on behalf of all the leaseholders and it is fair that they should pay any legal costs. But suppose the freeholder were involved in legal proceedings against one of the leaseholders: if the leaseholder lost, he would probably to be ordered to pay the freeholder's costs as well as his own; but if the freeholder lost, and had to pay both his own and the leaseholder's costs, he could simply, under the previous law, recover the money as part of the management element in the service charge. This meant that the freeholder was able to pursue legal action against leaseholders without fear of heavy legal costs in the event of defeat, the very factor that deters most people from too ready a resort to law. To prevent this, section 20C allows leaseholders to seek an order that the freeholder's legal costs must not be counted towards service charges.

Service charges held on trust: Section 42 of the Landlord and Tenant Act 1987 further strengthened the position of leaseholders by laying down that the freeholder, or the freeholder's agent, must hold service charge monies in a suitable interest-bearing trust fund that will ensure that the money is protected and cannot be seized by the freeholder's creditors if the freeholder goes bankrupt or into liquidation. However, public sector freeholders, notably local authorities and registered housing associations, are exempt from this requirement.

Administration charges: These are the freeholder's costs incurred in complying with leaseholders' requests for information and approvals under the terms of the lease. All such charges must be reasonable. Any demand for administration charges must be accompanied by a summary of leaseholders' rights and obligations in relation to them. The LVT has the power to decide whether or not an administration charge is payable, and if so, to whom and by whom together with the amount, date payable and the manner in which it is paid.

Ground rent: Strictly, this is not part of the service charge but as it is usually collected along with it, it is covered here. It will be specified in the lease and is usually a fairly modest annual sum in the order of £50 or £100. Leaseholders should note that, unlike the service charge and most other charges, the ground rent is not intended to compensate the freeholder for any costs or trouble; it is simply a payment by which the leaseholder recognises that ultimately the property belongs to the freeholder. Therefore freeholders are under no obligation to demonstrate that it is reasonable. But it is not payable unless the landlord has issued a formal request for it, which must specify the amount of the payment, the date on which the leaseholder is liable to pay it and the date (if different) on which it would have been payable under the lease. The date for payment must be at least 30 days and not more than 60 days after the date of the notice.

Insurance: Usually, any insurance required under the lease will be taken out by the freeholder and this is discussed below. Occasionally, however, the leaseholder will be required to take out insurance with a company nominated by the freeholder. If the leaseholder thinks he is getting a poor deal, he can apply to the county court or a Leasehold Valuation Tribunal which, if satisfied that the insurance is unsatisfactory or the premiums are unreasonably high, can order the freeholder to nominate another insurer.

'Period of Grace': When a dwelling is sold under the right to buy by a local authority or non-charitable housing association, the purchaser is given an estimate of service charges for the following five years. This estimate is the maximum recoverable during that time. Some purchasers under the right to buy have, however, had a very rude shock when the five year period of grace expires - see *Exceptionally High Service Charges* below.

d: The role of a recognised tenants' association

The tenants who are liable to pay for the provision of services may, if they wish, form a recognised tenants' association (RTA) under section 29 of the Landlord and Tenant Act 1985. Note that leaseholders count as tenants for this purpose (see Chapter One, where it explained that legally the two terms are interchangeable). If the freeholder refuses to give a notice recognising the RTA, it may apply for recognition to any member of the local Rent Assessment Committee panel ('Rent Assessment Committee' is the official term for a Leasehold Valuation Tribunal when it is carrying out certain functions, not otherwise relevant to leaseholders, under the Rent Act 1977).

An important benefit of having a RTA is that it has the right, at the beginning of the consultation process, to recommend persons or organisations that should be invited to submit estimates. However, the freeholder is under no obligation to accept these recommendations.

Another advantage is that the RTA can, whether the freeholder likes it or not, appoint a qualified surveyor to advise on matters relating to service charges. The surveyor has extensive rights to inspect the freeholder's documentation and take copies, and can enforce these rights in court if necessary.

Against these benefits must be set the principal disadvantage of having a RTA, namely that it weakens the freeholder's obligation to consult individual leaseholders. Where there is a RTA, the freeholder, instead of having to supply copies of the estimates to all leaseholders (or place copies where they are likely to be seen), merely has to send them to the secretary of the RTA, and the individual leaseholders must make do with summaries.

Leaseholders - and for that matter, ordinary periodic tenants - should therefore weigh carefully the advantages and disadvantages of setting up a RTA. If they decide against, there is nothing to prevent them from forming an ***unrecognised*** tenants' (or leaseholders') association, which can represent their interests to the freeholder, provided that it is made clear that formal recognition under section 29 is not being sought.

Challenging Service Charges

The Landlord and Tenant Act not only allows leaseholders to take action against unreasonable behaviour by the freeholder; it also enables them to take the initiative. This is done in two ways: by giving leaseholders rights to demand information, and by allowing them to challenge the reasonableness of the charge.

Any demand for service charges must include details about leaseholders' rights and how they can challenge the charges. If this is not done the leaseholder may withhold payment without penalty.

a: Right to information

Freeholders must provide a written summary of costs counting towards the service charge. It must be sent to the leaseholder within six months of the end of the period it covers. The service charge need not be paid until the summary is provided.

The law lays down some minimum requirements for the summary. It must:

- cover all the costs incurred during the twelve months it covers, even if they were included in service charge bills of an earlier or later period (see above for late charging and pre-charging);
- show how the costs incurred by the freeholder are reflected in the service charges paid, or to be paid, by leaseholders;
- say whether it includes any work covered by a grant (see above);
- distinguish: (a) those costs incurred for which the freeholder was not billed during the period; (b) those for which he was billed and did not pay; (c) those for which he paid bills.

If it covers five or more dwellings, the summary must, in addition, be certified by a qualified accountant as being a fair summary, complying with the Act, and supported by appropriate documentation.

The purpose of these rules is to put leaseholders in a position to challenge their service charges. After receiving the summary, the leaseholder has six months in which to ask the freeholder to make facilities available so that he can inspect the documents supporting the summary (bills, receipts, and so on) and take copies or extracts. The freeholder must make the facilities available within 21 days after such a request; the inspection itself must be free, although the freeholder can make a reasonable charge for the copies and extracts. Failure to provide these facilities, like failure to supply the summary, is punishable by a fine of up to £2500.

Very similar rules apply where the lease allows, or requires, the freeholder to take out insurance against certain contingencies, such as major repair, and to recover the premiums through the service charge. This is not unreasonable in itself and will, indeed, often be in the interests of leaseholders. The danger is, however, that the freeholder, knowing that the premiums are, in effect, being paid by someone else, has no incentive to shop around for the best deal. Section 30A of the Landlord and Tenant Act 1985 therefore lays down that leaseholders, or the secretary of the recognised tenants' association if there is one, may ask the freeholder for information about the policy. Failure to supply it, or to make facilities to inspect relevant documents available if requested to do so, is an offence incurring a fine of up to £2500.

It must be acknowledged that the rules allowing leaseholders to require information about service charges are, particularly in view of the £2500 fines, fairly onerous from the freeholder's point of view. It is the purpose of this book to inform leaseholders of their rights, not to make life difficult for freeholders: nevertheless, it must be admitted that if leaseholders wish to pursue a policy of confronting freeholders, and to cause them as much trouble as possible, sections 21, 22, and 30A offer plenty of scope.

b: Challenging a service charge

Any leaseholder liable to pay a service charge, and for that matter any freeholder levying one, may refer the charge to a Leasehold Valuation Tribunal to determine its reasonableness. This may be done at any time, even when the service in question is merely a proposal by the freeholder (for instance, for future major works). But the LVT will not consider a service charge if:

- it has already been approved by a court; or

- if the leaseholder has agreed to refer it to arbitration; or
- if the leaseholder has agreed it.

The first of these exceptions is obvious and the second is unlikely to apply very often. The third one is the problem: leaseholders should be careful, in their dealings with freeholders, to say or do nothing that could be taken to imply that they agree with any service charge that is in any way doubtful.

The LVT will consider:

- whether a service charge is payable and if so when, how, and by whom;
- whether the freeholder's costs of services, repairs, maintenance, insurance, or management are reasonably incurred;
- whether the services or works are of a reasonable standard; and
- whether any payment required in advance is reasonable.

The fees for application to a LVT can be obtained from the LVT and will usually change annually. Appeal against a LVT decision is not to the courts but to the Lands Tribunal.

By section 19 of the Landlord and Tenant Act 1985, any service charge deemed unreasonable by the LVT is irrecoverable by the freeholder. The determination of service charges by the LVT also plays an important part in the rules governing the use of forfeiture to recover service charges. It is to this that we now turn.

Forfeiture for Unpaid Service Charges

Forfeiture was mentioned at the end of Chapter Two. Briefly, it is the right of the freeholder to resume possession of the property if the leaseholder breaches the lease.

By section 81 of the Housing Act 1996, as amended by the 2002 Leasehold and Commonhold Reform Act, forfeiture for an unpaid service charge is available to the freeholder only if:

- the leaseholder has agreed the charge; or
- the charge has been upheld through post-dispute arbitration or by the Leasehold Valuation Tribunal or a court.

Regarding the first of these, it is necessary only to reiterate the warning to leaseholders to say or do nothing that could possibly be construed as representing their agreement to any service charge about whose legitimacy they have the slightest doubt.

Regarding the second, it should be noted that where the leaseholder has not agreed the service charge, proceedings before the LVT or a court or post-dispute arbitration are necessary before the freeholder can forfeit the lease.

A further requirement is that the amount of money involved must either exceed a certain amount or have been outstanding for a minimum period of time. The Government will set these limits by order. It is currently proposed that the minimum amount will be £350 and the minimum period three years, but this is yet to be confirmed. Note that it is necessary for only one of the requirements to be satisfied.

To sum up, before the freeholder can forfeit:
- it must have been formally decided that the service charge is due,
- the amount must exceed the minimum amount or have been owed for the minimum time, and
- a section 146 notice must have been served (but this requirement does not apply if the service charge is reserved as rent).

The freeholder can still begin the process by issuing a section 146 notice but it must state that the forfeiture cannot proceed until the requirements of section 81 have been met.

It remains to be seen how these new provisions will operate in practice. Their purpose is to prevent freeholders from using the draconian threat of forfeiture to pressurise leaseholders into paying disputed service charges, and to this extent the position of leaseholders has been greatly strengthened. The danger is that freeholders may respond by getting disputed charges before the LVT as quickly as possible so that forfeiture becomes available if the charges are upheld. Another concern is that some leaseholders, faced with service charges they are unwilling to pay but about which there is no dispute, may be unable to resist the temptation to invent spurious grounds for objection in order to deprive the freeholder of the weapon of forfeiture; this tactic is likely to provoke even relatively easy-going freeholders into legal action.

Once the leaseholder has agreed the service charge or it has been upheld by the LVT or a court or through arbitration, forfeiture becomes a serious threat and in this situation the advice can only be to pay the charge if at all possible. If, however, the leaseholder is unable to pay he may find it helpful to contact his mortgagee (if any). For the mortgagee, forfeiture is a disaster because it is likely to be left with a large unsecured debt on its hands, so many mortgagees in this situation will pay the service charges and add the cost to the outstanding mortgage. This does not solve the leaseholder's long term problem - that his lease commits him to payments he is unable to meet - but it will give him a little breathing space and may enable him to sell up and pay off his debts.

Some leaseholders, especially those of longer standing, may be living on fixed incomes and have very little cash to spare, even though their property is quite valuable. Sometimes their mortgage has been paid off altogether; even if it is still outstanding, it will probably be very small in relation to the value of the property. Leaseholders that find themselves in this 'property-rich, cash-poor' situation may find it helpful to look at equity release schemes, operated by a number of financial institutions.

11

Enfranchisement and Extension of Leases

What Are Enfranchisement and Extension?
Chapter One set out the legal theory underlying the relationship between freeholder and leaseholder, and explained that a lease must be limited in time and that, in principle, at the end of that time the lease finishes and the property reverts to the freeholder.

It has always been, and still is, open to the freeholder and the leaseholder to negotiate some different arrangement. For instance, they might agree that the freeholder will buy the unexpired term of the lease from the leaseholder: but, because the freeholder and the leaseholder cannot be the same person, this will have the effect of extinguishing the lease and the leave the freeholder on sole possession of the land as if the lease had never existed. Alternatively, the freeholder might agree to sell the freehold to the leaseholder: again, and for the same reason, this will extinguish the lease, but this time it is the former leaseholder that will be left in sole freehold possession. The sale of the freehold to the leaseholder is called 'enfranchisement' of the lease, because it is freed, or 'enfranchised', from the overriding freehold, and replaces it. A further possibility is that the freeholder and leaseholder may agree to extend the lease beyond its original term. If agreements of this kind are negotiated, it is entirely for the freeholder and leaseholder to settle the conditions and the price.

In recent years, however, the law has forced freeholders, in certain circumstances, to sell freeholds or extend leases, whether they wish to or not. This has been done by three pieces of legislation: the Leasehold Reform Act 1967, the Landlord and Tenant Act 1987, and the Leasehold Reform, Housing and Urban Development Act 1993 (although all three Acts have been amended by later legislation, particularly the Housing Act 1996 and the Commonhold and Leasehold Reform Act 2002). The Acts are dealt with in the order they were passed, which means that the most important right - that of leaseholders of flats - is left to last. This is fitting, because, as is explained below, it was a Parliamentary afterthought; the Government originally had no intention of granting such an important right.

But before looking at the legislation, it is important to establish why extension and enfranchisement are important to the average leaseholder.

Extension of a Lease Some enlightened freeholders automatically extend the lease whenever it is assigned, so that if a lease that was originally granted for 125 years is assigned after 30, the assignee gets a lease not for 95 years, as one might expect, but for 125. From the leaseholder's point of view, such an arrangement is extremely valuable because otherwise the lease represents a wasting asset, whose value will drop sharply as the end of the term approaches. The arrangement can also benefit the freeholder by making the lease more valuable at the time of its original sale. But most leases are unaffected by assignment and would expire on the originally determined date were it not for legislation that obliges freeholders, in certain circumstances, to grant a fresh 90 year lease to the leaseholder: this is described below.

Individual Enfranchisement of a lease Legislation, described below, now allows the leaseholder to acquire the freehold, in certain circumstances, whether or not the freeholder agrees. If not for this, the leaseholder would find that his home had reverted to the ownership of the freeholder at the end the lease and he would have to buy it back (assuming the freeholder were willing to sell). The freeholder is, however, entitled to compensation.

Collective Enfranchisement of Leases The problem with leasehold enfranchisement is that the property concerned must be capable of being held on a freehold basis. Where it stands on a distinct and definable piece of land this does not present a problem: the freehold of the land is transferred to the leaseholder and, as explained in Chapter One, any buildings on it are automatically transferred too. But if the property is only part of a larger building, it may not be attached to its own unique piece of land in the same way, so individual enfranchisement is not available to flat owners. If they wish to enfranchise, therefore, they have to agree among themselves that a single person or body will buy the freehold on behalf of all of them, while they continue to hold leases of their individual flats.

This is called 'collective enfranchisement', although this term is misleading because technically the leases have not been enfranchised at all: all that has happened is a change from the original freeholder to a new one nominated by the leaseholders. Since the passage of the Commonhold and Leasehold Reform Act 2002, this new freeholder has to be a special type of organisation called a 'Right to Enfranchise' (or 'RtE') company.

Rights to Enfranchise and Extend Leases: General Principles

The remainder of this Chapter sets out what rights leaseholders have if they wish to extend or enfranchise their leases. It is stressed at the outset, however, that anyone contemplating such a step should obtain independent legal advice from a solicitor, and in most cases also from a valuer. This applies not only if the lease is being enfranchised or extended under one of the Acts, but also if it is being done voluntarily by agreement with the freeholder. The issues involved are potentially very complex and attempting to deal with them without expert advice could put your home at risk.

The Acts are available to what they describe as 'qualifying tenants': but the exact meaning of the term varies depending which right is being exercised under which Act. Usually, but not always, the term is defined in a way that excludes ordinary tenants and confines it to leaseholders. The key issue is the existence of a long lease (see below). Other former tests, relating to residence or the amount of rent, were abolished by the 2002 Act.

A Long Lease For most purposes under the Acts, the leaseholder must own a lease originally granted for at least 21 years. Note that this is the term when the lease was granted, not the period it still has to run, so that a 99 year lease granted in 1910 is still a long lease in

2003 even though it has only six years to go. Recent legislation has put an end to a number of devices formerly inserted into leases by freeholders in order to avoid having to extend or enfranchise leases.

Some were bizarre: leases were made terminable on extraneous events, such as royal marriages or deaths, because the lease was not regarded as long if it depended on an event that could occur at any time. These evasions have been of no effect since the 1993 Act, which provides that leases containing them shall be treated as long leases.

Exemptions There are various exemptions from the Acts.
-    If the freeholder is a charitable housing trust and the dwelling is provided as part of its charitable work, the leaseholder can neither extend nor enfranchise the lease (unless the charity agrees).
-    The Acts do not apply to business leases. This applies even if a dwelling is included: for instance, if the lease of a shop includes the flat above it.
-    The Acts do not apply if the property is within the precincts of a cathedral or owned by the Crown (however, it is possible that the Crown authorities will agree to a voluntary extension or enfranchisement of the lease). Some properties owned by the National Trust are also exempt.
-    Other exemptions apply not across the board but to particular types of transaction. These are covered as the various Acts are discussed below.

Leasehold Reform Act 1967: Leases of Houses
The first legislation to deal with leasehold extension and enfranchisement was the Leasehold Reform Act 1967. This Act is still in force, but is not relevant to most residential leaseholders, who will get more benefit from later legislation. It can therefore be dealt with fairly briefly.

The Act relates only to residential leases of houses - not flats. With certain exceptions, a leaseholder qualifies to use it if he has held for at least two years a lease originally granted for 21 years or more. The Act allows qualifying leaseholders to acquire the freehold of their homes, or, if they prefer, extend the lease for 50 years.

The usual exemptions (see above) apply to the 1967 Act. In addition, it does not apply to most shared ownership leases granted by housing associations.

Most leaseholders qualifying to make use of the 1967 Act have long since done so, because the benefits of owning the freehold outweigh the drawback of having to pay the freeholder the difference (usually not very great) between the freehold and leasehold value of the house.

Generally speaking, therefore, remaining leasehold houses will be those to which the Act does not apply, either because the freeholder is exempt or because the house is attached to other property. The last point is an important limitation on the 1967 Act: if the land on which the house stands is shared by any other property not covered by the lease, however small it may be compared with the house, the Act cannot be used. It may, however, be possible for the leaseholder of such a house to use the new rights in the Leasehold Reform, Housing and Urban Development Act 1993.

The procedure for enfranchisement under the 1967 Act is as follows.

- The leaseholder serves a notice on the freeholder stating that he wishes to claim the freehold (or extend the lease). This notice should give particulars of the property and the lease.

- Within two months, the freeholder must send a counter notice that either accepts the leaseholder's claim or gives reasons for rejecting it. The freeholder may ask the leaseholder for a deposit of £25 or thrice the annual ground rent, whichever is more, and for proof that he holds the lease and meets the residence test. The leaseholder has 14 days to produce the money and 21 days to produce the proof.

- If the freeholder does not submit a counter notice within two months, the leaseholder's claim is automatically accepted. If the freeholder's counter notice unfairly rejects the leaseholder's claim, the leaseholder may apply to the county court.

Obviously, the freeholder is justified in rejecting the claim if the property does not come under the Act or if the leaseholder does not qualify. In addition, the freeholder may reject the claim if he acquired the house before 18th February 1966 and needs the house, on expiry of the lease, as a home for himself or a member of his family. He may also refuse to extend the lease (but not to enfranchise it) if he plans to redevelop the property.

Once it has been established that the leaseholder may enfranchise, a price must be agreed; if this is not possible, it will be set by a leasehold valuation tribunal. The Act lays down that the price should be the value of the freehold if it were being sold willingly but on the assumption that the lease were continuing and would be renewable under the Act. In effect, this formula means that the leaseholder is obliged to pay for what he is acquiring (the freehold) but not for what he has already got (the lease). Once a price has been agreed, or set by tribunal, either the freeholder or the leaseholder has one month to serve a notice on the other requiring him to complete. The freeholder must convey the freehold as a fee simple absolute, or (as a non-lawyer would say) outright.

Landlord and Tenant Act 1987: First Refusal and Mismanagement
The Landlord and Tenant Act 1987 was chiefly concerned with enabling leaseholders to protect themselves against unreasonable service charges, and it made numerous amendments to tighten the rules originally laid down in the Landlord and Tenant Act 1985 (see Chapter Three).

In addition, it granted leaseholders the important right of first refusal if the freehold of their property is sold. It also allowed leaseholders to acquire the freehold if the property is being mismanaged: however, this right is little used because of the difficult procedures involved, and although it remains on the statute book it is likely to fall into complete disuse because the 1993 Act has now given leaseholders the same right without having to prove mismanagement.

111

a: First refusal

The right of first refusal was granted in order to stop the practice of selling freeholds, without any reference to the leaseholders or other occupiers, from one person or organisation to another so that leaseholders were often completely in the dark about who the ultimate freeholder was (when this sort of thing went on the eventual freeholder often turned out to be a company existing on paper only and based somewhere completely inaccessible like the Cayman Islands - see Chapter Two for legislation passed at the same time forcing freeholders to give their name and an address in the UK for the service of legal notices). The right of first refusal remains important because it is sometimes available when ordinary collective enfranchisement, under the 1993 Act, is not possible.

The 1987 Act says that if the freeholder intends to sell the freehold he must first offer it to the leaseholders and other qualifying tenants. There are, however, some exceptions: the Act does not apply if the freeholder is selling to a member of his family, or if he lives in the block himself; nor does it apply if the block is not chiefly residential. In addition, virtually all public sector freeholders are excluded from the Act: this means local authorities, registered housing associations, and various other bodies. It is, however, unlikely that this sort of body will wish to sell its freehold. But if none of these exceptions applies, and if the majority of qualifying tenants (including leaseholders) wish to buy, they must be given the opportunity to meet the freeholder's price. For the purpose of defining a 'majority' there can be only one qualifying tenant in respect of each flat: in other words, joint tenants (or joint leaseholders) have only one 'vote' between them, and must agree between themselves how it will be used.

'Qualifying tenants' are:

- tenants entitled to a Fair Rent under the 1977 Rent Act: that is, most tenants of self-contained dwellings holding a tenancy originally granted on or before 14th January 1989, but excluding council tenants; and
- leaseholders, except for business leaseholders (the normal 21 year minimum does not apply).

If the qualifying tenants and freeholder cannot agree terms for the sale, the freeholder is able to sell to someone else. However, the qualifying tenants must be informed of this sale and, most importantly, of the price. They then have the right to buy the freehold from the new owner at whatever price he paid. This is designed to stop the original freeholder from asking the qualifying tenants for an excessive price that they are bound to reject, then selling to someone else at a lower price. Similarly, if the freeholder carries out a sale without informing the qualifying tenants, they have the right to buy from the new freeholder for the same price that he paid. Procedure under the 1987 for the right of first refusal is as follows.

* The freeholder notifies all qualifying tenants of his desire to sell and of the price at which he is willing to do so (including any non-monetary element). The notice must state the proposed method of sale: for instance, by conveyance or by auction.

* The freeholder must give the qualifying tenants at least two months to respond; and, if they say they wish to buy, at least a further two months (28 days if the sale is to be by auction) to come up with a nominee purchaser to acquire the freehold on their behalf. This could conceivably be in an individual or an organisation that already exists, but is much likelier to be a company set up specially for the purpose by the qualifying tenants, and under their control.

* During this period, the landlord and the qualifying tenants may wish to take the opportunity to negotiate the price.

* If a majority of the qualifying tenants have put forward a nominee purchaser and agreed with the freeholder on a price, the freeholder may not sell to anyone else.

* If the qualifying tenants fail to put forward a nominee purchaser, or if a mutually acceptable price is not agreed, the

freeholder has twelve months to sell to someone else in accordance with the original notice (by auction, if that was the method specified; and in any other case for a price not less than that originally offered to the qualifying tenants). If no sale has taken place within twelve months, the freeholder must start the procedure again from scratch if he wishes to sell.

b: Mismanagement: the right to enfranchise

As mentioned above, the 1987 Act is designed mainly to protect leaseholders against mismanagement and sharp practice by freeholders. It therefore gives them the power of collective enfranchisement against a freeholder guilty of serious or repeated breach of his obligations. The power is available to long leaseholders, but a leaseholder does not qualify to use this part of the Act if he owns long leases of three or more flats in the block.

Moreover, this part of the 1987 Act does not apply where the freeholder is the Crown or a public body such as a local authority or a registered housing association. Nor does it apply when the freeholder resides in the property himself. It is available only where two-thirds or more of the flats in the block are let on long leases, and in blocks of ten flats or fewer a higher proportion is required. The court can make an order transferring the freehold to the leaseholders' nominee only if a manager appointed (see Chapter Two) by a court or LVT has controlled the premises for at least two years, unless the leaseholders can show both

- that the freeholder is and is likely to remain in breach of his obligations under the lease; and
- that the mere appointment of a manager would be an inadequate remedy.

All these restrictions suggest that the Act envisages that enfranchisement on grounds of mismanagement is very much a last resort; indeed, it is necessary for the leaseholders to take their case to court and get permission before they can proceed. The right was seldom used and, although it remains available in theory, in practice it has been superseded by the 1993 Act, which gives most leaseholders the right of collective enfranchisement whatever the standard of management and with no need for a court order. Nevertheless, it is just possible there is a body of leaseholders somewhere willing to use the 1987 Act rather than the 1993 Act. The procedures for collective enfranchisement following mismanagement are therefore briefly set out here, with a warning that the general recommendation to employ a solicitor applies with special emphasis if this route is chosen.

- At least two-thirds of the qualifying leaseholders must serve a preliminary notice informing the freeholder that they intend to go to court to acquire the freehold. The notice must give the names and addresses of the leaseholder and the grounds for their application; the freeholder should also be given a reasonable deadline to rectify the problems if it is possible for him to do so.

- The leaseholders must apply to the court, giving their reasons for dissatisfaction and requesting an order to transfer the freehold to their nominee purchaser (probably, as with other forms of collective enfranchisement, a company set up for the purpose).

- If satisfied that it is fair to do so, the court will transfer the block to the nominee purchaser. The price will have to be agreed by the leaseholders and the freeholder; or, if (as is likely) this is not possible, by a Leasehold Valuation Tribunal. The price will be the value of the freehold on the assumption that all the leases are to continue: there will be no additional 'marriage value' (see below), and this is one of the few reasons for preferring to use the 1987 Act rather than the 1993 Act.

Leasehold Reform, Housing and Urban Development Act 1993: Collective Enfranchisement and Lease Extension

The 1993 Act greatly extended the rights of leaseholders: its passage through Parliament was, indeed, strongly contested by large private freeholders, who claimed that it was unfair to them as property owners. It made a number of adjustments, dealt with above, to existing rights under the 1967 and 1987 Acts; in addition, it created

115

two new rights for leaseholders of flats. These are the right to collective enfranchisement, and the right to extend individual leases.

a: Collective enfranchisement under the 1993 Act
In outline, the right to collective enfranchisement under the 1993 Act is similar to, but much easier than, collective enfranchisement under the 1987 Act. Under both schemes, qualifying leaseholders choose a purchaser to whom the freeholder can be forced to sell; but under the 1993 Act there is no need for a court order and no need to show that there has been mismanagement.

The 1993 Act is available to long leaseholders, provided that at least two-thirds of the flats are let on long leases and at least half the eligible leaseholders are involved.

However, the block may not be enfranchised if it falls within the normal exemptions, or if it is not chiefly residential, or if it is a house converted into four flats or fewer with a resident freeholder who owned the freehold before the conversion. Even if there is a resident freeholder, however, the scheme applies to houses converted into five flats or more and to purpose-built blocks even if they contain only two flats.

There are special provisions for any parts of the building that are occupied by people or organisations other than qualifying leaseholders. Some flats may be let to periodic tenants, for instance, and a block that faces a main road may well contain shop units on the ground floor. Any such parts may, and in some cases must, be leased back to the original freeholder when the block is acquired. 'Leaseback', as it is called, is mandatory for any flats let to periodic tenants (secure or assured) by a local authority or a registered housing association. This means that they can continue as council (or association) tenants, and do not lose any legal rights. It is up to the freeholder (not the leaseholders) whether he wants a leaseback of other flats or premises, such as business units or flats occupied by non-qualifying leaseholders. Unless the parties agree otherwise, leaseback is for 999 years at a notional rent - in other words, on terms typical of residential leases, and discussed in Chapters One and Two.

The leaseholders must choose a purchaser. Formerly, this could be any individual or organisation that had the confidence of the others and was willing to undertake the role. The 2002 Act has, however, tightened the rules by providing that only a 'Right to Enfranchise' ('RtE') company can take over the freehold. This protects leaseholders' rights by ensuring that the enfranchisee is a body in which they all have a right to be involved, but the Government has taken powers to lay down what the constitution of the RtE company must be, and it is likely that many leaseholders will find the prescribed constitution unwieldy and inflexible.

Setting up and running the RtE company is only one of the responsibilities in which collective enfranchisement will involve leaseholders. They will also have to pay both their own and the freeholder's legal and professional costs. And above all, they must pay the purchase price of the freehold, which, unless they come to an agreement with the freeholder, will be decided by a leasehold valuation tribunal in accordance with rules laid down in the Act. These say that the price consists of two components: the open market value and the 'marriage value'.

According to the formula in the Act, the **open market value** should reflect the income the freeholder would have received from rents plus the prospect of regaining possession of the parts of the building currently let. How much this is will depend on how the building is being used now. If, as will often be the case, it consists wholly of flats let on long leases with many years to run, the open market value will probably be low because ground rents are usually very modest and the prospect of regaining possession is a distant one and of correspondingly little value. But if the building contains lucrative business or periodic tenancies, perhaps quite short term, and if the freeholder elects not to have these leased back, the open market value will be substantial.

The other component in the price, the **'marriage value'**, is based on the assumption that, combined (as they will be after enfranchisement), the leases and the freehold have a greater value than they would if sold separately. The Act says the freeholder is entitled to half this amount. In most cases, however, especially where the leases have a long time to run, the marriage value will be low, and where a lease has more than 80 years to run the marriage

117

value will be disregarded. Altogether the costs of enfranchisement may be considerable. It is therefore prudent for leaseholders to explore the ground before committing themselves. This can be done by any qualifying leaseholder by serving a notice on the freeholder (or whomever the leaseholder pays rent to) under section 11 of the Act. Such a notice obliges the freeholder to disclose, within 28 days, information that will be relevant to any sale, such as title deeds, surveyor's reports, planning restrictions, and so on. This will allow the leaseholders to take an informed view of whether they wish to go for collective enfranchisement and, if so, on what terms. At this stage, they should take their time and think it over carefully, for if they proceed further they will be obliged to pay the freeholder's legal costs if they later decide to withdraw.

It may be appropriate, too, at this stage, for the leaseholders to ask the freeholder whether he is prepared to consider a voluntary sale without forcing all concerned to go through the somewhat elaborate procedures laid down by the 1993 Act. A reasonable freeholder, since he will be aware that he can be forced to sell anyway, may well be willing to discuss this.

If the leaseholders decide to go ahead with collective enfranchisement under the 1993 Act, they must form a 'Right to Enfranchise' ('RtE') company. The purpose of the company is to act as the vehicle for the enfranchisement and subsequently to own the freehold of the block.

Every RtE company has to operate in accordance with a constitution (the 'memorandum and articles') laid down by Government. The aim is to ensure that all leaseholders have a fair chance to take part, but it is likely that many leaseholders will find that the constitution laid down for them is extremely bureaucratic and unwieldy, especially when it is remembered that many enfranchisements will be carried out in small blocks where they may be only a dozen leaseholders or even fewer.

All qualifying leaseholders are entitled to be members of the RtE company, but in practice it is controlled by 'participating members', namely those leaseholders that have served on the company a 'participation notice'. When the company is set up all qualifying leaseholders must be sent a formal notice inviting them to participate by serving such a notice. Once the enfranchisement takes place, membership of the RtE company is confined to participating members.

The RtE company serves an initial notice (also called a 'section 13 notice') giving the names and addresses of the leaseholders involved and exactly specifying what property they wish to enfranchise and which parts, if any, they will lease back. The notice must also propose a price, and give the freeholder at least two months to reply. Once the initial notice has been served, the freeholder may not sell the freehold to any third party.

From now on, the RtE company handles proceedings on behalf of the leaseholders. The freeholder may require the RtE company to provide evidence to show that the participating leaseholders are qualified under the Act. If the RtE company does not respond within 21 days, the freeholder may in some circumstances treat the initial notice as being withdrawn.

By the date specified in the initial notice, the freeholder must serve a counter notice either accepting the leaseholders' right to enfranchise or giving reasons for rejecting it. The freeholder must also state whether he accepts the details of the leaseholders' proposal as regards price and exactly what is to be included in the sale, and must say whether he wishes to lease back any parts of the property (in addition to those where leaseback is mandatory). The freeholder may refuse to exercise his right to lease back parts of the premises let on lucrative business lets because the effect of this will be to increase the price and, perhaps, deter the leaseholders from continuing. In the unlikely event that most of the leaseholders' leases have less than five years to run, the freeholder has the right to stop the enfranchisement if he can satisfy a court that he intends to redevelop the block.

The intention of the Act is that after the freeholder's counter notice the parties will attempt to resolve any differences, so that the sale of the freehold can proceed on agreed terms. Often, however, agreement will be impossible and in that case the matters in dispute are referred to a leasehold valuation tribunal. Such a referral must take place at least two months, and not more than six months, after the freeholder's counter notice; if no agreement is reached, and no referral made, after six months, the initial notice will be deemed withdrawn.

Once the terms have been settled, the parties have two months to exchange contracts. At the end of this time, the nominee purchaser has a further two months to ask a court to transfer the freehold on the terms agreed (or determined by the tribunal); or the freeholder may ask the court to rule that the initial notice shall be treated as being withdrawn.

To sum up, the procedure is complex and demanding, which is why it has been little used even though several years have passed since it became available under the 1993 Act. The 2002 Act has made the process more favourable to leaseholders in some ways, but these improvements are more than offset by the further layer of difficulty added by the new requirement to set up a RtE company. All in all, it seems likely that these procedures will not be much used, but their existence may be helpful in persuading freeholders to negotiate seriously if leaseholders want to buy the freehold.

b: Lease extension under the 1993 Act

Although the right to collective enfranchisement, as created by the 1993 Act, is of great importance because it makes a fundamental shift in the relationship between freeholders and leaseholders, the complex procedures mean that it is likely to be relatively seldom used. On the other hand, the right to a new lease, which was also created (for flat owners) by the 1993 Act, is likely to prove of immense practical benefit to thousands of leaseholders, not least because it can be exercised on an individual basis. It is ironic that this, the most valuable right leaseholders derive from the 1993 Act, was something of a Parliamentary afterthought. The original intention was to create the right to collective enfranchisement, with individual lease extensions as very much a second best option available only to leaseholders that for some reason were disqualified from collective enfranchisement. But as the legislation made its way through Parliament the right to extend leases was granted to more and more categories of leaseholder, and by the time the Act became law it had become a general right.

The principle is similar to the right to lease extension that house owners enjoy under the 1967 Act. Anyone that has owned for at least two years a long lease of a flat qualifies to extend it under the 1993 Act. The former low rent test and residence test were abolished by the 2002 Act. The freeholder is required to grant a new lease running for the remainder of the term of the old lease plus an additional 90 years, so that if the old lease had 40 years to go the new one will be granted for 130. In other respects, however, the terms of the new lease will be the same as, or very similar to, the old one.

The leaseholder will have to pay the freeholder a sum consisting of two components calculated in accordance with rules set out in the Act. The first represents the reduction in the market value of the freehold that results because the freeholder will now have to wait to regain possession for 90 years longer than would otherwise have been the case. The less time the old lease had to run, the higher this component is likely to be. The second component is the 'marriage value', reflecting the higher value of a longer lease. As with collective enfranchisement, the freeholder is entitled to 50% of the marriage value, but it is disregarded altogether if the old lease has more than 80 years to go.

A leaseholder who is contemplating a lease extension should begin by serving a preliminary notice on the freeholder. This has the same function as with collective enfranchisement: it commits the leaseholder to nothing, but requires the freeholder to supply within 28 days the information that will enable the leaseholder to decide whether to go ahead.

The procedure is modelled on that for collective enfranchisement:

- The leaseholder serves an initial notice (a 'section 42 notice') on the freeholder. This must give details of the property concerned as well as of the leaseholder and his claim to qualify to use the 1993 Act. It must state how much the leaseholder proposes to pay, and set a date, at least two months ahead, by which the freeholder must reply. Once the notice has been served, the leaseholder must allow the freeholder to have access to the flat for the purpose of valuation.

- The freeholder must either agree that the leaseholder qualifies under the Act, or give reasons for disagreeing. If the freeholder agrees that the leaseholder is qualified to extend the lease, he may still suggest a that price of the new lease, or its other terms, should be different to the leaseholder's proposals. The freeholder can go to court for permission to reject the extension entirely if the current lease has less than five years to run and the freeholder then intends to redevelop the property.

- The freeholder and leaseholder should then attempt to resolve any differences by negotiation. If agreement is not reached, the question may be referred to the leasehold valuation tribunal at lease two months, and not less than six months, after the freeholder's counter notice. If, six months after the counter notice, there is neither an agreement nor a referral to a tribunal, the leaseholder's initial notice will be deemed withdrawn. In this event the leaseholder is liable for any reasonable expenses incurred by the freeholder.

- Once the terms are settled, either by negotiation or by the tribunal, the parties have two months to exchange contracts. If exchange does not take place during this period, the leaseholder has a further two months to apply to court for an order extending the lease on the terms agreed (or laid down by a tribunal).

It should be noted that collective enfranchisement takes priority over individual lease extensions, so that the effect of an initial notice of collective enfranchisement is to freeze, for the time being, any current claims to extend leases. If the collective enfranchisement fails to go ahead, the extension claims resume where they left off.

12

Business Tenancies

Business tenancies

A business tenancy is the same as any other tenancy with the exception that it is governed by the 1954 Landlord and Tenant Act. To be eligible for protection as a business tenant the occupier must fall within the definition provided by section 23 of the 1954 Act which states:

1) Subject to the provisions of this Act, this part of the Act applies to any tenancy where the property comprised in the tenancy is or includes premises which are occupied by the tenant and are so occupied for the purposes of a business carried on by him or for those and other purposes.

A person will be a business tenant if he or she has a tenancy of that premises, occupies a part of the premises and the premises are occupied solely for the purposes of carrying on a business.

A business tenancy may be periodic or fixed term. A sub-tenant will also be protected. However, a licence to occupy will not be protected under the 1954 Act. The principles of Street v Mountford will apply with business tenancies. By merely wording what is in reality a tenancy a licence, the landlord cannot escape the provisions of the 1954 Act. However, it was highlighted in the case Dresden Estates Ltd v Collinson (1987) 1 EGLR 45 that 'the attributes of a residential premises and a business premises are often quite different' and that 'the indicia, which may make it more apparent in the case of a residential occupier that he is in fact a tenant may be less applicable or be less likely to have that effect in the case of some business tenancies'. In this case, the landlord retained the right to move the tenant to a different premises. This was held to be inconsistent with the right of exclusive possession and therefore inconsistent with the existence of a tenancy.

Business premises

The word premises, to describe business premises, is used in a wider sense. For example, a piece of land leased for training horses has been construed as a business premises (Bracey v Read 1963 CH 88).

Occupation for the purposes of a business

A tenant must occupy a property or part of a property to gain protection under the 1954 Act. In addition the tenant must also occupy for the purposes of a business. Business is defined by s23(2) of the Act:

1) In this part of the Act the expression 'business' includes a trade. Profession or employment and includes any activity carried on by a body of persons, whether corporate or unincorporated.

There is a difference created here between an individual business tenant and a corporate tenant. For an individual to fall into the category of business tenant, he or she will have to carry out an activity that can be classed as a trade, profession or employment. One case highlights this Lewis v Weldcrest (1978) 3 ALL ER 1226, Mrs Lewis took in lodgers but gained no real quantifiable commercial advantage from doing so. The courts held that the facts did not amount to a trade. The whole distinction is a matter of degree, to what degree is a business being carried on?

Corporate tenant

S 23(1A) has been inserted into the 1954 Act to clarify the position where premises are occupied by a company as opposed to an individual. Under s23A occupation or the carrying on of a business:

a) by a company to which the tenant has a controlling interest; or

b) where the tenant is a company, by a person with a controlling interest in the company shall be treated as equivalent to occupation or the carrying on of a business by a tenant.

The tenant as a body of persons

Where the above is the case the statute seems to indicate that any activity will count as business purposes. One example is where the trustees of a tennis club took the tenancy of tennis courts and a club house, the activity of the tennis club was held to be a business purpose within the 1954 Act (Addiscombe Garden estates Ltd v Crabe (1958) 1 QB 513. However, the scope of the word 'activity' should not be regarded as infinite. In Hillil Property v Naraine Pharmacy (1980) 39 P&CR 67 Megaw LJ stated:

'Though an activity is something that is not strictly a trade, a profession or employment, nevertheless to be an activity for this purpose it must be something that is correlative to the conceptions involved in these words'.

Mixed business and residential use

Statutory codes applying to business tenancies and residential tenancies are regarded as mutually exclusive. For the 1954 Act to apply the business use of a premises must be a significant purpose of the tenant's occupation of the premises. This is not always an easy question to determine. At one end of the scale is the tenant who works nine to five on the premises. On the other there are many examples in between. The doctor who runs a surgery away from home but who sees patients in his flat and the businessman who conducts an import export business from home. Both of these situations were considered in two appeals which were heard together Cheryl Investments Ltd v Saldanha and Royal Life Savings Society v Page (1978) 1 WLR 1329 and which throw light on the legal status of mixed residential and business use.

The doctor in Royal Life Savings had his consulting rooms in Harley Street. By entering into a tenancy of the maisonette where he lived he had asked for, and been granted, by the landlord, permission to carry on his profession there. Both addresses appeared in the medical directory and both phone numbers put on stationary. However, in practice, the doctor very rarely saw patients at his maisonette. The court held that the professional use of the maisonette was incidental to the business and that the doctor has a Rent Act protected tenancy of the maisonette.

In Cheryl Investments, on the other hand the businessman had installed a telephone and installed other business equipment in his flat. The business was solely operating from these premises. The courts held that in this case the occupation of the flat was for a significant business purpose and was therefore a business tenancy.

Breach of covenant

If a business tenant is carrying on a business at a premises which is in breach of either a general covenant against business user or in breach of a covenant against use for the purposes of trade, profession or employment, then that tenancy will not normally fall within the 1954 Act. There are a number of situations, however, where it will come under the Act, even where there is a breach of covenant:

a) if the covenant extends to only part of the premises
b) if the covenant prohibits use only for a specified business
c) If the covenant allows only a specific business

A tenancy will also come under the Act if the landlord has consented to the breach.

Exclusions from the 1954 Act

Certain tenancies are expressly excluded from the 1954 Act:

a) agricultural holdings and farm tenancies
b) mining leases
c) tenancies of premises licensed to sell alcohol, not including hotels and restaurants and other premises where the sale of alcohol is not the main use of the premises, which were granted before 11th July 1989. Tenancies of premises

licensed to sell alcohol granted after this date do fall within the Act,

d) service tenancies (for employment which lasts as long as the job). If the tenancy was granted after 1st October 1954, the tenancy the tenancy must have been granted in writing clearly expressing the purposes for which the tenancy was granted.

e) Short tenancies granted for a term certain and not exceeding six months unless the tenancy contains provisions for extending it beyond six months.

Contracting out of the 1954 Act

The Regulatory Reform (Business Tenancies) (England and Wales) Order 2003 inserted a new provision into the 1954 Act, being s38A which allows a landlord and tenant to enter into an agreement that the provisions relating to security of tenure will not apply to a tenancy. In order for an agreement of this kind to be valid, the landlord must serve on the tenant a notice in a prescribed form. This notice will state that the tenancy is excluded from the provisions set out in ss24-28 relating to security. The provisions of s38 will only apply to agreements entered into after 1st June 2004. For agreements entered into before this date then the parties to the tenancy must ask the courts to authorise the agreement.

Security of tenure under the 1954 Act

S24 of the LTA 1954, as amended, contains the core provisions relating to security of tenure. The basis of security is that of automatic continuation of the tenancy. A tenancy that comes under the act will not come to an end unless it is terminated in one of the ways set out in the act. S24 provides:

1) A tenancy to which this part of the Act applies shall not come to an end unless terminated in accordance with the provisions of this part of the Act and, subject to the following provisions of this Act either the tenant or the landlord under such a tenancy may apply to the court for an order for the grant of a new tenancy-

a) if the landlord has given notice under s 25 of this Act to terminate the tenancy or

b) if the tenant has made a request for a new tenancy in accordance with s26 of this Act.

This section has been amended by the Regulatory Reform (Business Tenancies) (England and Wales) Order 2003. Before this amendment it was only the tenant whop could make an application under s24.

Thus the method used by the LTA 1954 to provide security of tenure acts to prevent the tenancy coming to an end in the first place. The tenancy continues as it did before the end of the contractual term and remains an interest in land that can be disposed of.

Termination of a business tenancy

There are a number of methods of termination under the LTA 1954. They can be divided into two categories, the common law methods of termination which are preserved by the Act and the statutory methods of termination as provided for in the Act. For common law methods of termination the 1954 Act s24 (2) provides:

2) The last foregoing subsection shall not prevent the coming to an end of a tenancy by notice to quit given by the tenant, by surrender or forfeiture or by the forfeiture of a superior tenancy unless-

a) in the case of a notice to quit, the notice had been given before the tenant had been in occupation in right of the tenancy for one month; or

b) in the case of an instrument of surrender, the instrument was executed before, or was executed in pursuance of an agreement made before, the tenant had been in occupation in right of the tenancy for one month.

Article 3(2) of the Regulatory Reform (Business Tenancies) (England and Wales) Order 2003 has added further provision to s24 (2) to take account of the fact that it is now possible for landlord or tenant to serve notice:

(2A) Neither the tenant nor the landlord may make an application under s 24(1) if the other has made such an application and that application has been served.
(2B) Neither the tenant nor the landlord may make such an application if the landlord has made an application under s29 (2) of this Act and the application has been served.
(2C) The landlord may not withdraw an application under s 24(1) unless the tenant consents to its withdrawal.

The aim of the 1954 Act is to protect the tenant from termination by the landlord. The tenant can still terminate the tenancy by serving a notice to quit. The tenant can also surrender the tenancy. The tenant cannot serve a notice to quit or surrender the tenancy before he or she has been in occupation for one month. The Act does not affect the landlord applying for forfeiture in the event of the tenant breaching the lease. The landlord must follow the strict provisions relating to application for forfeiture.

Statutory methods of termination
Under the 1954 Act there are four ways that a tenancy to which the act applies can be brought to an end:

a) by the landlord giving notice to terminate the tenancy under s25;
b) by the tenant making an application for a new tenancy under s26;
c) by the tenant giving notice to terminate the tenancy under s 27(2);
d) by the landlord and tenant agreeing a new tenancy under s28.

Business use ceases after the fixed terms expires

If a tenant ceases to use the premises for business purposes after the contractual term has expired and while the tenancy is being continued by s24 (1) then the tenancy ceases to be protected by the 1954 Act. The tenancy does not automatically come to an end however. Section 24(3)(a) provides that the landlord may terminate the tenancy by not less than three or not more than six months notice in writing to the tenant.

If a tenant commences business user following a notice in writing this does not affect the operation of the notice.

Competent landlord

The 1954 LTA provides a mechanism for identifying the landlord with whom the tenant should deal. This landlord is known as the 'competent' landlord. Only a competent landlord can serve a tenant a notice to terminate a tenancy under s 25 of the Act. The competent landlord is not always the immediate landlord.

Section 44(1) 0f the Act provides that the competent landlord will be either:

a) the owner of the fee simple: or
b) the landlord lowest in the chain of tenancies who has a tenancy which will not come to an end within 14 months by effluxion of time, and no notice has been given which will end the tenancy within 14 months.

Agreement for a new tenancy

Section 28 of the 1954 Act provides that when a competent landlord and a tenant enter into an agreement for the grant of a tenancy at a future date and the agreement specifies the terms and date of commencement of the tenancy:

a) the current tenancy will continue until that date but no longer: and
b) the current tenancy ceases to be the one to which pt 11 pf the 1954 Act applies

Termination by the landlord

In order to terminate a tenancy to which the 1954 Act applies, the landlord must serve a notice in accordance with s25. By serving such a notice the landlord puts in motion the mechanisms of the renewal procedure. This is based on a series of time limits. The notice must be given in the prescribed form and must:

a) specify the date at which the tenancy must come to an end
b) require the tenant, within two months of giving the notice, to notify the landlord in writing, whether or not, at the date of termination, the tenant will be willing to give up the tenancy of the property
c) state whether the landlord would oppose the granting of a new tenancy

From 1st June 2004, notice should be given of Form 1 if the landlord does not oppose the grant or Form 2 if opposed, of the LTA 1954 Part 2 (Notices) Regulations 2004 (S1 2004/1005). Prior to this date the landlord may have drafted his or her own notice.

Once a valid s 25 notice has been served the landlord has no power to amend it. A notice can only be withdrawn in very limited circumstances where, within two months of serving it, a superior landlord becomes the competent landlord.

Timing of the s25 notice

The notice must be given not more than 12 or less than six months before the date of termination specified in the notice. Where a landlord wishes to terminate a business tenancy the date has to be clearly specified in the notice. How the date is calculated will depend on whether the tenancy is fixed term or periodic.

Periodic tenancies

At common law, a periodic tenancy is normally brought to an end by notice to quit. Under the 1954 Act the date of termination given in the notice must not be earlier than the earliest date upon which the tenancy could have been brought to an end at common law by a notice to quit. At common law, it is necessary that the NTQ expires

131

on the anniversary of the tenancy. Under the 1954 Act the landlord does not have to be so precise, provide that the date of termination given by the landlord is later than the date at which the tenancy could be terminated by NTQ. The notice, however, must be given not more than 12 months or less than six months before the date of termination specified in the notice.

Fixed term tenancies
With fixed term tenancies the date of termination is easier to calculate. The earliest date of termination is the date upon which the tenancy would have come to an end by effluxion of time if it had not been continued by s24 of the LTA 1954. The earliest point at which a landlord can serve a notice under s 25 is one year before the tenancy is due to expire. In every case the landlord must give at least six months notice even once the contractual tenancy is expired and the tenancy is being continued under s 24 of the LTA 1954.

A considerable number of business tenancies, however, allow termination before the expiry of the term by incorporating a break clause into the agreement. The question here is whether the landlord has to serve two notices to terminate the tenancy, one under s25 and one which follows the contractual provisions under the break clause.

If s25 notice can be served that follows the provisions of the Act and also fulfils the criteria set out in the break clause, then this will suffice and one notice is sufficient. One case that highlighted this was Scholl Manufacturing Co Ltd v Clifton (Slim Line) Ltd (1967) 3 ALL ER 16. In practice, a landlord will often serve two notices to safeguard the situation and ensure an effective ending.

If a landlord serves a notice that satisfies the provisions of s25 but does not satisfy the provisions of the break clause then the s25 notice will be of no effect. However, if the landlord serves a notice that satisfies the break clause but not s25 then the tenancy will come to an end. However, the tenancy continues under s24 until the landlord complies with the provisions of the Act.

Termination by the tenant

The tenant cannot end the tenancy simply by giving up possession of the property on the last day of the fixed term. Notice must be served by the tenant or obligations will continue under the agreement. If the tenant has actually quit then the tenancy ceases to be protected by the Act and the tenancy will end. However, in other circumstances procedures under the Act must be followed.

There are two ways in which a tenant can bring a business tenancy to an end under the 1954 Act:

a) by requesting a new tenancy under s26
b) by giving notice under s27.

The first of these options is applicable where the tenant does not wish to give up the tenancy. The second is applicable where the tenant wishes to end the tenancy. It is rarer for a tenant to request a new tenancy under s26 than it is for a landlord to apply to terminate the tenancy under s25. Until the landlord indicates that he or she wants to end the tenancy it will not usually be in the tenants interest to request a new one. The tenancy will be continued anyway under s 24 and will probably be on more favourable terms to the tenant than a new one.

On the other hand it is usually in the interests of the landlord to terminate the tenancy under s 25 even if the landlord does not want to regain possession, as it is the opportunity to grant a new tenancy on more favourable terms to the landlord.

Who can request a new tenancy?

Not every tenant can take advantage of s26 of the 1954 Act. The tenant must hold a tenancy which is either a tenancy granted for a term of years certain exceeding one year (whether or not continued by s24) or a tenancy granted for term certain and thereafter from year to year.

Neither the holder of a periodic tenancy nor a fixed term tenancy of less than one year can request a new tenancy under s 26. Periodic tenants and holders of fixed term tenancies of less than one year can still apply for a new tenancy if a landlord serves them with a section 25 notice. It should be noted that the holder of a fixed term tenancy of less than six months will be excluded from the Act by s 43(3).

There are provisions in the 1954 Act designed to prevent the operation of s26 clashing with the operation of s25 or s27. If the landlord has already served a s25 notice, the tenant cannot then request a new tenancy under s 26. Similarly, if the tenant has already served notice under s27 he or she cannot subsequently request a new tenancy under s26.

The contents of a s26 notice
The tenant's request for a new tenancy has to be served on the competent landlord. It must be set out in the prescribed form (s26 (3) and set out the tenant's proposals as to the property to be comprised in the tenancy, the rent payable and the terms of the new tenancy. A date of commencement of the new tenancy should also be specified.

From 1st June the prescribed form is Form 3 of the Landlord and Tenant Act 1954, Part 2 (Notices) Regulations 2004. Prior to this date notice should have been given on Form 8 of the Landlord and Tenant Act 1954 Pt 11 (Notices) Regulations 1983.

The date of commencement of the new tenancy must not be more than six months or less than six months after the date of the request. The date must not be earlier than that which would bring the tenancy to an end by the effluxion of time or could be brought to an end by notice to quit given by the tenant.

The effect of a s26 notice is to terminate the current tenancy immediately before the date specified in the request for a new tenancy. Section 64 of the Act provides for the interim continuation of the tenancy until the application of a new tenancy is disposed of. If the new tenancy is not taken up by the tenant s 26(2) allows for a short continuation of the interim tenancy whilst parties to the tenancy sort out their affairs.

Once a tenant has served a s26 notice it is not possible to withdraw it and serve a second request.

The timescales applicable to a s26 request are similar to a s25 notice given by a landlord. Once the landlord has received the notice he or she has two months to serve notice on the tenant that an application will be made to court to oppose the grant of a new tenancy s26 (6). There is no prescribed form for the landlords notice in opposition, but it must state on which of the grounds set out in s30 of the 1954 Act the landlord will oppose the application. If the landlord fails to serve the notice of opposition then he or she will lose the right to oppose the tenant's application for anew tenancy. They will, however, still be able to argue the terms of a new tenancy.

Termination by tenants notice under s 27

This second method of termination applies when the tenant does not wish to apply for a new tenancy. It is applicable only in the case of fixed term tenancies. S27 can only be used once the tenant has been in occupation for more than one month. Where a tenant is continuing by virtue of s24 then three months notice can be given to the landlord.

S23 of the Landlord and Tenant Act sets out rules governing service of notice. Notices must be in writing and can be served personally or sent to the last known place of abode in England or Wales of the person to be served. Place of abode also means place of business. An authorised agent can also serve notice.

It should be noted that even if a notice which is invalid because of some deficiency within, it may be deemed to be valid by virtue of being accepted by the person receiving it. Once accepted, the person waives or may waive the right to claim that the notice is invalid. Therefore, the lesson here is always read the contents of the notice. One such case that highlights this is Keepers and Governors of the Possessions Revenues and Goods of the Free Grammar School of John Lyon v Mayhew(1997) 1 EGLR 88 CA.

A tenants application for a new business tenancy

A business tenants right to apply to the courts for a new tenancy is enshrined in the 1954 Act and is one of the main purposes of the Act. A new tenancy can only be granted upon termination of the old tenancy. The right to apply for a new tenancy will only arise in two circumstances:

a) where the landlord had terminated the current tenancy by serving a s25 notice;

b) where the tenant has terminated the current tenancy by requesting a new tenancy under s26.

A business tenant will have no right to apply for a new tenancy where the tenant has chosen to relinquish his ort her tenancy by serving notice under s 27.

The 1954 Act encourages the landlord and tenant to reach agreement. By serving a notice a statutory framework is created. This framework requires the parties to set out their intentions and reasons within a time frame. If agreement is not reached within the timescales then the tenant can apply to court for the matter to be settled and the landlord can apply to the court for an interim rent to be fixed.

The courts powers to order the grant of a new tenancy or to terminate a tenancy are contained within ss 29 to 31 of the 1954 Act. Some amendments have been made to these provisions by the Regulatory Reform (Business Tenancies) (England and Wales) Order 2003. A new section 29A has been added which amends the time limits for the making of an application. Under the new provisions any application made by a tenant or landlord under s24 (1) or by a landlord under s 29(2) (for the termination of a tenancy without renewal) must be made before the end of the statutory period. This is the period ending:

a) where the landlord gives notice under s25 of the act on the date specified in the notice; and

b) Where the tenant has made a request for a new tenancy under s 26 immediately before the date specified in his request.

The time limit may be extended by agreement between the parties.

Procedure

A claim for a new tenancy should be made under the procedure set out in part 8 of the Civil Procedure Rules 1999. Such a claim is subject to the modifications introduced by pt 56(3) of the CPR. No claim made after 15th October 2002 should be made without reference to pt 56.

The landlord opposing the grant of a new tenancy

The Landlord and Tenant Act 1954 ss30 (1) provides seven grounds upon which the landlord may oppose a tenant's application for a new tenancy. If the landlord wishes to rely upon any of these grounds then he or she must state them either in the s25 notice or in the landlords counter notice to the tenant's s26 request. Once a ground has been specified this cannot be changed. If a landlord specifies a ground and subsequently sells the interest then the new landlord can only rely on the ground specified by the original landlord (Marks v British waterways Board (1963) 3 ALL ER 28 CA.

The following are the grounds:

Ground (a) – tenants failure to comply with repair obligations

The landlord must establish that the premises under the tenancy are in a state of disrepair as a result of the tenant's failure to comply with the repairing obligations under the lease. The landlord must demonstrate that the breaches are serious enough for the court not to grant a new tenancy. The court will consider the severity of the breach and also the tenant's willingness to rectify the breach, plus the tenants past conduct. A case which highlights this is Lyons V Central Commercial properties Ltd (1958) 2 ALL ER 767.

Ground (b) Tenants persistent delay in paying rent
The landlord must establish that the tenant has a history of non-payment. Occasional delays are not enough. Nor will the fact that there are currently outstanding arrears amount to persistent delay. A number of factors are taken into account including:

a) Whether the delay cause the landlord inconvenience and expense
b) Whether the tenant can offer a good explanation for the delay and show that it was exceptional
c) Whether the tenant can ensure future payment, for example by providing a deposit or by offering to pay interest in any future arrears (Rawashdeh v land (1988) 2 EGLR 109 CA.

Ground (c) – Tenants breaches of other obligations or uses of the holdings.
This ground covers breaches of obligations by the tenant other than rent or disrepair. The landlord must show that there has been a substantial breach.

Ground (d) – suitable alternative accommodation available
A court has no discretion over this ground if the landlord can demonstrate that suitable alternative accommodation at a similar term and use is available.

Ground (e) – Landlord requires whole property for subsequent letting
This comes into effect when the landlord has let premises and the tenant has sub-let part of the premises requires the whole for letting. This arises very rarely indeed.

Ground (f) – landlord intends to demolish or reconstruct the premises
This is one of the most common grounds used. A Landlord intending to rely ion this ground must demonstrate a real intention to demolish or reconstruct not just a mere desire to do so. The landlord also needs to demonstrate that he or she needs possession,

legally as well as physically, to be able to reasonably carry out the works. If the landlord is able to enter and carry out the works with the tenant in-situ, under a covenant in the tenancy agreement, then the landlord will not be able to succeed under this ground. One such case demonstrating this is Heath v Drown (1973) 2 ALL ER 561.

Even where, under the terms of the current tenancy, the landlord is able to show that he or she requires possession of the holding, the landlord may still fail to succeed under ground (f). Section 31(A) of the 1954 Act, inserted by s 7(1) of the Law of Property Act 1969, provides that in two situations the court will order a new tenancy:

(a) the tenant agrees to the inclusion in the terms of the new tenancy of terms giving the landlord access and other facilities for carrying out the work intended and given that access and those facilities, the landlord could reasonably carry out the work without obtaining possession and without interfering to a substantial extent or for a substantial time with the use of the holding of the business carried ion buy the tenant or:

(b) the tenant is willing to accept a tenancy of an economically separable part of the holding and either paragraph (a) of this section is satisfied with respect to that part or possession of the remainder of the holding would be reasonably sufficient to enable the landlord to carry out the intended work.

Ground (g) – landlord intends to occupy the building

Section 30 (2) of the 1954 Act provides that a landlord cannot rely on this ground if the landlord's interest was purchased or created after the beginning of the period of five years, which ends with the termination of the current tenancy. Therefore, the landlord must have owned the interest for five years. The aim of this provision is to prevent a landlord buying an interest with the aim of going into occupation himself.

The landlord will have to establish a real intention. This is a question of fact. The landlord does not have to show that he or she intends to occupy the premises him or her self. In Parkes v Westminster Roman Catholic Diocese Trustee (1978) 36 P&CR 22 it was held that the Trustees could occupy through the agency of a parish priest. Occupation through a management company is also sufficient.

The effect of opposition

If the landlord successfully establishes any of the above grounds in s 30(1) to the satisfaction of the court then the court cannot order the grant of a new tenancy. Where a landlord seeks to rely on Ground (d) (e) or (f) (suitable alternative accommodation, uneconomic sub-tenancy, intention to demolish or reconstruct) but fails to establish the ground to the satisfaction of the court, s 31(2) offers a further chance of obtaining possession:

Section 31(2) provides that:

(2).... If the court would have been satisfied of any of these grounds if the date of termination specified in the landlords notice or, as the case may be, the date specified in the tenants request for a new tenancy as the date from which the new tenancy is to begin, had been such later date as the court may determine, being a date not more than one year later than the date so specified-

(a) the court shall make a declaration to that effect, stating on which of the said grounds the court would have been satisfied as aforesaid but shall not make an order for the grant of a new tenancy;

(b) if, within 14 days after the making of the declaration, the tenant so requires the court shall make an order substituting the said date for the date specified in the said landlords notice or tenants request, and thereupon that notice or request shall have effect accordingly.

The tenants right to be compensated

Where a landlord opposes a tenant's application for a new tenancy under grounds (a) (b) or (c), the basis of the opposition is that the tenant has breached some part of the tenancy. In the case of ground

(d) there is no loss to the tenant because suitable alternative accommodation is provided in exchange for the original tenancy. Grounds (e) (f) and (g) however, are not upon the default of the tenant but on the needs of the landlord. Section 37 of the 1954 Act (as amended) therefore gives the tenant a right to compensation where the landlord has served notice opposing the grant of a tenancy under any one of these grounds. Section 37 will apply where:

(a) the tenant has applied for a new tenancy under s 24(1) and the landlord has successfully opposed the application under (e) (f) or (g); or
(b) the landlord has specified these grounds in his or her application for the termination of a tenancy under s 29(2) and the court has been unable to grant a new tenancy by reason of any of these grounds; or
(c) the landlord has specified grounds (e) (f) or (g) in his or her notice and the tenant has either not applied for a new tenancy or has made a new application but has subsequently withdrawn it.

The amount of compensation due to a tenant is calculated by multiplying the rateable value of the holding by an appropriate multiplier. The rateable value for this purpose is the RV fixed at the time of the service of notice. The multiplier is fixed by the Secretary of State. Longer standing business will attract a higher rate of compensation.

Compensation for misrepresentation
A new s 37A has been added to the 1954 Act by the Regulatory Reform (Business Tenancies) (England and Wales) Order 2003. This section enables a tenant to claim compensation from the landlord if the tenant has not applied for a new tenancy, or has not been granted a new tenancy because the landlord has misrepresented facts to the tenant or the court, or has concealed material facts. The damages will be calculated to compensate the

tenant for any loss or damage sustained because of the refusal of the grant of the new tenancy, including leaving the premises.

Where a s25 notice has been served the tenancy will continue automatically until a date three months after the application has finally been disposed of. either through conclusion of court proceedings or through withdrawal of tenant's application.

Determination of an interim rent

Between the time of serving a s25 or s 26 notice and the final grant of a tenancy, there may be considerable delay. During this time the tenant or landlord may apply for the determination of an interim rent. The application must be made within six months of the termination of the old tenancy. The provisions governing the application and determination of the interim rent are contained in the new s24A to 24D of the 1954 Act. These sections have been substituted in place of the old s 24A by Article 14 of the Regulatory Reform (Business tenancies) (England and Wales) Order 2003.

The amount of rent

In most cases, if the landlord and tenant have agreed that a new tenancy will be granted, the amount of rent payable under the new tenancy will also be the interim rent. If the landlord or tenant can show that the interim rent should be different the court can order this different rent to be paid. If the landlord and tenant have not agreed then the courts can determine an interim rent. In making the determination, the court will have regard to the rent payable under the terms of the tenancy and the rent payable under any sub-tenancy of part of the property, but otherwise the court should determine the rent as it would be under s34 (1) and (2) as if a new periodic yearly tenancy were to be granted of the whole building. The rent will be determined with regard to the current state of repair of the building, even if the repair is due to a breach of the tenancy Fawkes v Viscount Chelsea (1980) QB 441 3 ALL ER 568.

The court can, in order to soften the blow of a large rent increase due to the difference between what the tenant is currently paying and the open market rent, order a lower interim rent. The interim rent will be payable from the earliest date that could have been specified in the notice.

Where a new tenancy is granted under the 1954 Act

Terms of the new tenancy

The court will determine the terms of the new tenancy where parties are unable to come to agreement. The courts will also resolve the matter of what property is included if this cannot be agreed. Normally the new tenancy will be the holding. If the parties are unable to agree what constitutes the holding then the court will decide this by reference to circumstances existing at the date of the order. In two situations the tenancy will not be of the holding:

(a) Where the landlord has opposed the grant of a new tenancy on ground (f) and by virtue of s 31A (1) the tenant has agreed to accept a tenancy of part of the holding, in which case the court will order the grant of a tenancy on that part only.

(b) Where by virtue of s 32 (2) the landlord requires the new tenancy to be the tenancy of the whole of the property comprised in the current tenancy.

Section 32(2) is of importance to a landlord where the tenant is not occupying the whole of the premises, for example where the premises includes a flat and the tenant has sub-let the flat. Under the 1954 Act the tenant only has the right to a new tenancy of the holding, i.e. the shop. In such a situation, the landlord may have no interest in recovering only the flat and can require that all of the property comprised in the current tenancy is included in the new tenancy. Section 32(3) further provides that where the current tenancy includes rights enjoyed by the tenant in connection in connection with the holding, those rights shall be included in the new tenancy unless the parties agree to the contrary. For example, in Re No 1 Albermarle Street W1 (1959) CH 531 (1959) 1 ALL ER 250 the tenant had a right to display advertising signs on the outside of the premises under his current tenancy and this right was included in the new tenancy.

The duration of the new tenancy

If the parties to the tenancy are unable to agree the length of a new tenancy then the court will determine the length. The new tenancy can either be for a fixed term or a periodic tenancy. If fixed, then it will be for a length no longer than 14 years. The court can also take into account the relative hardship caused either party.

Rent

The most contentious area, usually, concerning business tenancies, is that of rent. When parties to a tenancy fail to reach agreement section 34 (1) of the 1954 Act provides that the rent payable under a business tenancy:

…..may be determined by the court to be that which, having regard to the terms of the tenancy (other than those relating to rent) the holding might reasonably be expected to be let in the open market to a willing lessor….

The court has wide discretion when assessing the open market rent. The court will rely on expert witnesses, such as surveyors, in most cases. If there are no recent comparables the court will look at the general increases in an area over a given period. The court will also take into account the terms of a tenancy. Where a court has to determine other terms of a tenancy then these will need to be considered before setting rent. One case that highlights this is Cardshops Ltd v Davies (1971) 2 ALL ER 721.

There are certain factors that will be ignored when setting rent:

a) Any effect on rent of the fact that the tenant or his predecessors in title have been in occupation of the holding. Time is not a determining factor.
b) Any goodwill attached to the holding by reason of the carrying on of the business of the tenant

c) Any effect on rent of an improvement. By s34 (2) the improvement must have been carried out by a person who was at that time the tenant and it must not have been carried out carried out in pursuance of an obligation to the current landlord. The improvement must have been carried out under the current tenancy or:

(1) it was completed not more than 21 years before the application for the new tenancy was made: and
(2) the holding or any part of it affected by the improvement has at all times since been comprised in tenancies to which pt11 of the 1954 Act applies: and
(3) at the termination of each of these tenancies the tenant did not quit.

By s 34(3) the court may, if it thinks fit, include a provision varying the rent. The court may therefore require a rent review clause to be included in the new tenancy.

Other terms in the tenancy
Other terms, if they cannot be agreed, can be determined by the court. In determining the terms the court shall have regard to the terms of the current tenancy and to all relevant circumstances (s35).

Where one party wishes to introduce new terms different to the existing terms in a tenancy, it is up to that person to show good reason for the change. One case that demonstrates this is O'May v City of London Real property Co Ltyd (1983) 2 AC 726. In this case the landlords wanted to introduce a term into the tenancy requiring the tenant to pay a service charge. The result of this change would be to shift the cost of repairs and maintenance onto the tenant. In return, a small reduction in rent was offered. The court held that this particular change was unjustified.

Where the court makes an order for a new tenancy the landlord and tenant are bound to accept the order, with the exception that of the parties to the tenancy both agree to ignore the order they are free to do this. Secondly, the tenant may apply to the court within 14 days of the order being made to have the order revoked s 36(2).

Compensation for improvements under the 1927 Act

Part 1 of the landlord and Tenant Act 1927 as modified by Pt 111 of the LTA 1954 contains provisions giving the tenant the right to claim compensation for certain improvements made to the premises when he or she quits the premises. The right is not very extensive and is limited to authorised improvements as specified by the Act.

The provisions of the 1927 Act apply only to holdings where the premises are held under a lease and are used wholly for trade or business and includes any under lease. Certain premises are excluded from the 1927 Act, premises let under mining lease and agricultural holdings, service tenancies if the tenancy was entered into after 1927 and is in writing, premises used to carry on a profession, where the profession is not regularly carried on at the premises and premises that are sub-let as residential flats.

The following improvements are not included for the purposes of compensation:

a) improvements made before the commencement of the Act
b) improvements begun before 1st October 1954 and were made in pursuance of a statutory obligation
c) improvements which tenants or successors in title were obligated to carry out in pursuance of a contract entered into for valuable consideration.

The tenant must follow a rigid procedure when carrying out the improvement and claiming compensation. The right to compensation does not arise automatically, the improvement must be authorised and pre-conditions laid out in the Act must be followed. As with all things, the whole process is notice driven.

The tenant's application should be made in the county court using CPR Pt 8 procedure. The new provisions contained in CPR Pt 56 and PD 56 set out the rules for the contents and form of the application.

Where an application is made to the court, the court must give a certificate if it is satisfied that:

a) the improvement is of such a nature as to be calculated to add to the letting value of the holding at the end of the tenancy;
b) the improvement is reasonable and suitable to the character of the holding;
c) the improvement will not diminish the value of any other property belonging to the landlord or to any superior landlord.

The court can also modify the proposed plans and specifications. The landlord can prevent a certificate being granted to the tenant if he or she offers to carry out the improvements themselves.

The amount of compensation

Section 1(1) of the 1927 Act provides that the amount of compensation shall not exceed:

a) the net addition to the value of the holding as a whole which may be determined to be a result of the improvement; or
b) the reasonable cost of carrying out the improvement at the termination of the tenancy subject to a deduction of an amount equal to the cost (if any) of putting the works constituting the improvement into a reasonable state of repair, except as so far as such cost is covered by the liability of the tenant under any covenant or agreement as to the repair of the premises.

Section 1(2) provides that in determining the amount under item (a), regard shall be had to the purposes to which it is intended that the premises shall be used after the termination of the tenancy. If it is shown that it is intended to demolish, or to make structural alterations to or to change the user of the premises, regard shall be had to the effect of these acts on the additional value attributable to the improvements, and to the length of time likely to elapse between the end of the tenancy and the demolition, alteration or change of use.

Section 2(3) provides that compensation should be reduced to take into consideration any benefits which the tenant or predecessor in title may have received from the landlord in consideration of the improvement.

Landlords can avoid the effect of the 1927 Act by putting in a covenant obliging the tenant to carry out any improvement to which the landlord agrees, putting in a covenant demanding reinstatement at the end of the tenancy and deciding to demolish or change use of the premises at the end of the tenancy. Since December 1953 it has not been possible for landlords and tenants to contract out of the provisions of the 1927 Act.

13

Agricultural Tenancies

The Agricultural Tenancies Act 1995 changed the nature of agricultural tenancies. From 1st September 1995, no more tenancies of 'agricultural holdings have been granted and agricultural tenancies came to be known as 'Farm Business tenancies' having much more in common with the 1954 LTA than it does with previous agricultural Acts such as the Agricultural Holdings Act of 1986. At its heart, the 1995 Act has the notion of freedom of contract. Parties are free to negotiate the tenancy on whatever terms suit them. The act imposes no more security of tenure beyond the length of the tenancy agreed between landlord and tenant. There are no rights of succession.

Definition of Farm Business Tenancy

A tenancy will be a farm business tenancy for the purposes of the 1995 Act if it meets the business conditions together with either the agricultural condition or the notice conditions (s1 (1) (a). It cannot be a farm business tenancy if it began before September 1st 1995 or if the tenancy is an agricultural holding, There are certain tenancies which may be agricultural holdings if they began after September 1st if they fall within the exceptions set out in s4. These include:

(a) where the tenancy begins after 1st September but pursuant to a written contract of tenancy entered into before that date which indicates that the 1986 Act is to apply in relation to that tenancy (s4 (1) (a);

(b) where the tenancy was obtained under the right of succession contained within the 1986 Act;: whether the tenancy was obtained by a direction of the ALT under s 39 or s53 of the 1986 Act, granted by the landlord under s 45 (6) of the 1986 Act following a direction of the ALT or granted by a written

149

contract of tenancy following an agreement with the landlord:

(c) where the tenancy was granted under the 'Evesham custom':

(d) where the tenancy was granted to someone who immediately before the grant was the tenant of the holding (or a substantial part of the holding under the 1986 Act and the new tenancy was not expressly granted but had effect as an implied surrender and re-grant of the tenancy though the purpose was only to vary the lease.

Business conditions

There are two business conditions:

(a) that all or part of the land comprised in the tenancy is farmed for the purposes of a trade or business, and

(b) that since the beginning of the tenancy all or part of the land has been so farmed.

Both conditions must be satisfied. The business conditions do not require that the same part of the land is always farmed for the purposes of a trade or business: they will be satisfied even if different parts of the land have been used for commercial farming at different times, provided that at all times some part of the land has been farmed for the purposes of a trade or business.

If during the course of a tenancy the land ceases to be used for agricultural activity, the business condition will cease to be satisfied and the tenancy will fall outside of the 1995 Act. However, if the land continues to be used for a commercial purposes then it may still qualify as a business tenancy under the 1954 LTA.

The agriculture condition

S 1 (3) of the 1995 Act states that the agricultural condition is that, having regard to:

(a) the terms of the tenancy
(b) the use of the land comprised in the tenancy
(c) the nature of any commercial activities carried on that land
(d) any other relevant circumstances

The character of the tenancy is primarily or wholly agricultural.

Unlike the business conditions, the agricultural conditions do not have to have been satisfied since the beginning of the tenancy, it only needs to have been satisfied since the beginning of the proceedings. However, it does require that the tenancy is primarily or wholly agricultural.

The notice conditions

The notice conditions make sure that the tenancy will remain a farm business tenancy. To satisfy the notice conditions there are two requirements. The first is that, on or before the relevant day, the landlord and tenant each gave each other a written notice:

(a) identifying the land to be comprised in the tenancy and:

(b) containing a statement to the effect that the person giving the notice intends the tenancy or proposed tenancy is to be, and remain, a farm business tenancy (s 1)4) (a)

The relevant day is defined in s 1(5) as whichever is the earlier of the following:

(a) the day on which the parties enter into any instrument creating the tenancy, other than an agreement to enter into a tenancy on a future date, or

(b) the beginning of the tenancy.

The second requirement is that, at the beginning of the tenancy the character of the tenancy was primarily or wholly agricultural (s 1 (4) (b). This requirement of the notice condition needs only to be satisfied at the beginning of the tenancy. Provided that notice has properly been served it does not matter if the tenancy moves away from agriculture. The tenancy will remain a farm business tenancy provided that a part of the land is used for agriculture.

Terminating a farm business tenancy

The ATA 1995 affords minimal security of tenure for farm business tenancies. The basic protection is given through the time periods imposed when serving notice to quit. These are contained within sections 5 6 and 7 of the Act. No grounds for possession are needed, unlike assured or secure tenancies.

Fixed term tenancies of two years or more:

Section 5 (1) provides that:

..A farm business tenancy for a term of two years or more shall, instead of terminating on the term date, continue (as from that date) as a tenancy from year to year but otherwise on the terms of the original tenancy so far as applicable, unless at least twelve months but not less than twenty four months before the term date a written notice has been given by either party to the other of his intention to terminate the tenancy.

As in the Agricultural Holding Act 1986, the 1995 Act ensures the continuation of longer-term fixed term tenancies. Such tenancies require a year's notice of termination. It is not possible to contract out of the provisions of s 5. The provisions apply to both landlord and tenant.

Fixed term tenancies of two years or less

These tenancies have no protection under the 1995 act and will expire at the end of the term.

Tenancies from year to year

Section 6 (1) of the 1995 Act provides:

Where a farm business tenancy is a tenancy from year to year, a notice to quit the holding or part of the holding shall be invalid unless:

(a) it is in writing
(b) it is to take effect at the end of a year of tenancy, and
(c) it is given at least twelve months but less than twenty-four months before the date on which it is to take effect.

Thus a tenancy from year to year will be subject to twelve months notice as a minimum.

Sub-tenants

The 1995 Act gives no protection to sub-tenants. If the head tenancy is terminated by notice to quit then sub-tenancies will also be terminated.

Joint tenants

If a landlord serves a notice to quit on any one of a number of sub-tenants, or one joint tenant serves notice to quit on the landlord, this will determine the joint tenancy.

Licensees

The 1995 Act offers no protection for licensees and they will fall outside its provisions. However, the rule laid out in street v Mountford will apply and any agreement purporting to be a licence which grants exclusive occupation at a rent will in fact be a tenancy.

Rent

The position with regard to rent in a farm business tenancy is determined by the law of contract, or the underlying principles of freedom of contract. The parties are free to agree between them what the level of rent should be and also periods for variation of rent. The Act does supply a mechanism for arbitration but also allows parties to opt out of these provisions. The statutory rent review provisions will not come into force where the tenancy agreement states that the remit will not be reviewed during the period, where the agreement states that tie rent will be varied at a specified time by a specified amount and also where ether agreement states that the rent shall be varied at specified times using a formula.

Statutory rent increase provisions

Under the 1995 Act, either the landlord or tenant can demand a rent review every three years. This is done by serving a statutory review notice on the other party requiring the rent to be referred to arbitration. The review date must be at least twelve months but less than 24 months after the day on which the statutory review notice is given. Where there is no agreement in writing, the review date will be the anniversary of the beginning of the tenancy unless the landlord and tenant agree in writing that it is to be some other date and the three year period will run from the latest of the following dates:

(a) the beginning of the new tenancy
(b) the date as from which there took effect a previous direction of an arbitrator as to the amount of rent
(c) the date as from which there took affect a previous agreement in writing between the landlord and tenant, entered into since the grant of tenancy, as to the amount of rent.

Even if there is an agreement in writing re the rent the matter can still be referred to tribunal.

Severance of the landlord's reversion

Section 11 makes special provisions with regard to the severance of the landlord's reversion. If the landlord sells part of his estate which is let to a tenant under a farm business tenancy and as a result of severing the estate a new tenancy of part of the land is granted to the tenant, the three year period between statutory rent reviews will run from the granting of tie original tenancy not from the creation of the new tenancy.

Compensation for improvements

Section 16 gives a farm business tenant the right, subject to certain conditions being fulfilled, to be entitled on the termination of the tenancy, to obtain from the landlord compensation for any tenants improvements s 16 (1). Tenant's improvements mean any physical improvement which is made on the holding by the tenant wholly or partly at his or her expense. It also means any intangible advantage which is obtained for the holding by the tenant by his own effort or wholly or partly at his own expense. The right does not arise in respect of any physical improvement which is removed from the holding or any intangible advantage which does not remain attached to the holding.

Compensation will only be available if the tenant has obtained landlords consent for improvements. The consent should be in writing s (17)1. If a landlord fails to give consent for an improvement, or fails within two months of the request in writing or requires the tenant to agree to a variation in terms as a condition of giving consent then the tenant may notify the landlord in writing that he or she wishes to apply for arbitration under s 19. s19 will only apply if the tenant gives notice in writing before commencing the improvement, except where the improvement is a routine improvement. This is defined as an improvement made in the normal course of farming the holding or any part of the building which does not consist of fixed equipment or an improvement to fixed equipment (s19(10).

Landlords consent for planning permission

Where planning permission is required for the tenants improvement special conditions apply regarding landlords consent. The tenant will only be entitled to compensation if:

(a) the landlord has given his consent in writing to the making of the application for planning permission and;

(b) that consent is expressed to be given for the purpose of enabling the tenant to make a specified physical improvement to the holding or of enabling the tenant lawfully to effect a specified change of use and;

(c) on the termination of the tenancy, the specified physical improvement has not been completed or the specified change of use has not been effected (s 18(11).

The amount of compensation for improvements will be an amount equal to the increase attributable to the improvement in the value of the holding at the termination of the tenancy. This amount will be reduced where the landlord has agreed to contribute part of the costs of improvements.

Protection of Residential Agricultural workers
So far, we have dealt with the commercial letting of agricultural land. However, a different area of law is the residential protection of agricultural workers. This is specifically where a premises is supplied as part of the job.

In order for an occupier to acquire an assured agricultural occupancy or protection under the Rent (Agriculture) Act 1976 it is an essential requirement that the premises is either arranged or owned by the occupier's employer.

This, however, will not always be the case. Many agricultural workers will be tenants like any other tenants and may acquire protection under the Housing Act 1988 or the Rent Act 1977 depending on when the tenancy was granted. The fact that they work in the field of agriculture will not make any difference.

The main Acts to be considered are the 1976 Rent (Agriculture) Act and Chapter 111 of the 1988 Housing Act.

The Rent (Agriculture) Act 1976
Tenancies and licences granted before 15th January 1989 will be governed by the Rent (Agriculture) Act 1976. In order to fall within

the protection of this Act a number of definitions must be satisfied. The agricultural worker must be a 'qualifying worker', the tenancy or licence must be a 'relevant' tenancy or licence and the dwelling house in question must be in 'qualifying ownership'.

Qualifying worker

A person is a qualifying worker for the purposes of the act at any time, if at that time he or she has worked for the whole time in agriculture for not less than ninety-one percent of the last 104 weeks (Sch 3 para 1). A person can also be within the protection of the Act if he or she is incapable of work because of a disease or accident arising as a result of their work.

Agriculture

'Agriculture' is defined by s 1 (1) of the 1976 Act to include dairy farming, livestock keeping and breeding, the production of any consumable produce and the use of land for grazing, pasture, orchards, market gardens, nurseries and forestry. This is not an exhaustive list. For example, a person employed to repair farm machinery is employed in agriculture (McPhail v Greensmith (1993) 2 EGLR 228 CA but a gamekeeper is not (Normanton (Earl of) v Giles (1980) 1 WLR 28 HL.

Relevant licence and relevant tenancy

A relevant tenancy is a tenancy of a separate dwelling which would be a protected tenancy under the Rent Act 1977 but for the provisions of the 1977 Act listed below. A relevant tenancy may not be a tenancy which falls under Part 11 of the Landlord and Tenant Act 1954 (business tenancies), part 1 of the 1954 Act or Sch 10 to the Local Government and Housing Act 1989 (long leases).

A relevant licence is any licence under which a person has the exclusive occupation of a dwelling house as a separate dwelling which, if it were a tenancy, would be a protected tenancy under the Rent Act 1977 but for the provisions of the 1977 Act listed below.

The provisions of the 1977 Rent Act are:

(a) s 5 (which excludes tenancies at low rents, see 13.44) (Sch 2 para 3(2)

(b) s 10 (which excludes a tenancy of a dwelling house which is comprised in an agricultural tenancy holding which is occupied by the person responsible for the control of the farming of the holding, see 13.65 (Sch 2, para 3(2).

(c) S 7 (which excludes a tenancy where the rent includes payment for board or attendance, see 13.51) The 1976 Act modifies this section to make it clear that meals provided in the course of a persons employment in agriculture do not constitute 'board' (Sch 2, para 3).

Protected occupier

Section 2(1) and (2) of the 1976 Act provide that a person will be a protected occupier in his or her own right (as opposed to by succession) where:

(a) he or she holds a relevant licence or a relevant tenancy in relation to a dwelling house, and

(b) the dwelling house is in qualifying ownership or has been in qualifying ownership at any time during the subsistence of the licence or tenancy (whether it was at the time a relevant licence or tenancy or not) and either:

(i)   he or she is a qualifying worker, or

(ii)   he or she has been a qualifying worker at any time during the subsistence of the licence or the tenancy (whether at the time it was a relevant licence or tenancy or not), or

(iii) he or she is incapable of whole time work in agriculture in consequence of a qualifying injury or disease.

Security of tenure

The system of security of tenure offered under the 1976 Act is very similar to that offered by the Rent Act 1977. S 4 (1) of the 1976 Act provides that when a protected occupiers tenancy or licence is terminated, and the tenant or licensee continues to occupy the dwelling house as his residence, a statutory tenancy will arise. The protected occupiers licence or tenancy may be terminated by a notice to quit, a notice of increase of rent under s 16(3) of the act or otherwise.

A court may not make an order for possession of a dwelling house subject to a protected tenancy or a statutory tenancy unless the landlord can establish one of the statutory grounds for possession set out in Sch 4 (s6 (1). As under the Rent Act 1977 these are divided into discretionary and mandatory grounds. In the case of discretionary grounds the court will not make an order for possession unless it considers it reasonable to do so. The court also has power to adjourn. It can also stay or suspend the execution of an order or postpone date of possession.

Discretionary Grounds under the 1976 Act:

1. That suitable alternative accommodation is, or will be available
2. That the housing authority has offered to provide or arrange suitable alternative accommodation
3. That the tenant has not paid rent lawfully due
4. That the tenant is guilty of annoyance or nuisance to neighbours
5. That the condition of the dwelling house has deteriorated due to the tenants actions
6. That the condition of furniture has deteriorated due to actions of the tenant
7. That the tenant has given notice to quit and the tenant would be seriously prejudiced if he could not obtain possession.
8. That the tenant has sub let or assigned without permission
9. That the dwelling house is reasonably required for occupation by the landlord
10. That the tenant is overcharging a sub-tenant.

Mandatory grounds

The landlord must show:

(a) that before granting the tenancy the person who granted the tenancy (the original occupier) occupied the dwelling house as his or her only or principal home and the court is now satisfied that the dwelling house is now required as a residence for the original occupier or member of family who lived with the original occupier when he or she last occupied the property and the original occupier gave notice to the tenant before the start of the tenancy that possession might be recovered under this case.

(b) That the person who granted the tenancy acquired the dwelling house with a view to occupying it as a residence on his or her retirement, that person has now retired and requires the dwelling house as his or her residence or that they have died and it is required for a member of the family and that notice was given to the tenant before the start of the tenancy that possession might be recovered under this case.

(c) That the dwelling house is overcrowded within the meaning of part X of the Housing Act 1985 in such circumstances as to render the occupier guilty of an offence.

Rent

With a protected tenancy in employment a low rent or no rent at all will usually be applicable. This will not the case when a protected tenancy is terminated and a statutory tenancy begins. Rent will only be payable when a statutory tenancy arises if the landlord and tenant fix the rent by agreement under s 11 of the Act or the landlord serves a notice of increase of rent under s 12 or s 14 of the act.

As under the Rent Act 1977, both parties have the right to apply to register a fair rent.

Succession

The 1976 Act provides for a single succession. Where the deceased was a protected occupier in his or her own right (i.e. not by succession) his or her spouse, providing he or she was resident with the tenant immediately before death, and has a relevant licence or tenancy, will succeed to the protected tenancy. If there is no spouse, a member of the deceased's family can succeed providing that they resided with the deceased six months before the death. Where the protected tenancy has been terminated and the deceased is a statutory tenant the situation is different. A spouse may succeed to a statutory tenancy as may a family member who has resided with the deceased for two years before death. However, a family member, in contrast to a spouse, will succeed to an assured tenancy under the Housing Act 1988.

Assured Agricultural occupancies

Tenancies and licences granted to agricultural workers after 125th January 1989 will be governed by Chapter 111 of the Housing Act 1988.

In order to be an assured agricultural occupancy the tenancy or licence of the dwelling house must be:

(a) an assured tenancy which is not an assured shorthold tenancy

(b) a tenancy which would be an assured tenancy but for the fact that it is excluded by:

(i) the provision of Sch1, para 3, 3A and 3B which exclude tenancies at low rent or

(ii) the provision of Sch1, para 7 which excludes a tenancy of a dwelling house which is comprised in an agricultural holding or farm business tenancy which is occupied by the person responsible for the control of the farming or management of the holding, or

(c) a licence under which a person has exclusive occupation of a dwelling house as a separate dwelling which, if it were a tenancy, would satisfy (a) or (b) above.

Agricultural worker condition

The first requirement of the agricultural worker condition is that the dwelling house must be in a qualifying ownership or have been in qualifying ownership at any time during the subsistence of the tenancy or licence (whether or not it was at that time a relevant tenancy or licence). Qualifying ownership is defined as under the 1976 Act.

The second requirement is that the occupier (or where there are joint occupiers at least one of them):

(a) is a qualifying worker or has been a qualifying worker at any time during the subsistence of the tenancy or licence (whether or not it was at that time a relevant tenancy or licence): or

(b) is incapable of whole time work (or work as a permit worker) in agriculture in consequence of a qualifying disease.

Where the agricultural worker condition is fulfilled and the tenant or licensee is granted another relevant tenancy or licence of another dwelling house in consideration of giving up possession of the original dwelling house, the tenant or licensee will continue to satisfy the agricultural worker condition.

Succession

The agricultural worker condition may also be fulfilled by succession. This will occur where a dwelling house is subject to a relevant tenancy or licence and an occupier who satisfied the agricultural worker condition has died. A spouse may succeed where she was residing with the deceased at the time of his or her death and, if there is no spouse, a member of the family may succeed if they were residing g with the deceased for the period of two years before his or her death.

Security of tenure

Where the tenancy or licence is a relevant tenancy or licence and the agricultural worker condition is fulfilled, the tenancy or licence will be an assured agricultural occupancy. An assured agricultural occupancy which is not an assured tenancy will be treated as if it were an assured tenancy (s24 (3) with the following alterations:

   (a) a landlord will not be entitled to seek possession of the dwelling house under ground 16

   (b) if the tenant gives notice to terminate his or her employment, that notice shall not constitute a notice to quit notwithstanding any agreement to the contrary

   (c) when an assured agricultural tenancy is terminated and a statutory periodic tenancy arises by virtue of s 5 that statutory periodic tenancy will be an assured agricultural occupancy as long as the agricultural condition is for the time being fulfilled with respect to the dwelling house in question

   (d) if no rent is payable under an assured agricultural occupancy the statutory tenancy that arises on termination of then occupancy will be a monthly periodic tenancy.

Assured shorthold tenancies

Since the introduction of assured shorthold tenancies in the 1988 Housing Act many agricultural workers have been granted shortholds which provides a simple way of gaining recovery of a property.

INDEX

Emerald Publishing
www.emeraldpublishing.co.uk

106 Ladysmith Road
Brighton BN2 4EG

Other titles in the Emerald Series:

Law
Guide to Bankruptcy
Conducting Your Own Court case
Guide to Consumer law
Creating a Will
Guide to Family Law
Guide to Employment Law
Guide to European Union Law
Guide to Health and Safety Law
Guide to Criminal Law
Guide to Landlord and Tenant Law
Guide to the English Legal System
Guide to Housing Law
Guide to Marriage and Divorce
Guide to The Civil Partnerships Act
Guide to The Law of Contract
The Path to Justice
You and Your Legal Rights

Health
Guide to Combating Child Obesity
Asthma Begins at Home

Emerald Ultimate Nutrition Guide for cancer Sufferers and Their Friends and family

Music
How to Survive and Succeed in the Music Industry

General
A Practical Guide to Obtaining probate
A Practical Guide to Residential Conveyancing
Writing The Perfect CV
Keeping Books and Accounts-A Small Business Guide
Business Start Up-A Guide for New Business
Finding Asperger Syndrome in the Family-A Book of Answers
A Guide to Dementia
Being a Professional Writer
For details of the above titles published by Emerald go to:

www.emeraldpublishing.co.uk